Alicia Alonso

ALICIA ALONSO
The Story of a Ballerina

BEATRICE SIEGEL

FREDERICK WARNE
NEW YORK LONDON

Frederick Warne & Co., Inc.
New York, New York

1   2   3   4   5   83   82   81   80   79

Printed in the U.S.A. by The Maple Press Company
Book design by Kathleen Westray

Library of Congress Cataloging in Publication Data
Siegel, Beatrice.
Alicia Alonso, the story of a ballerina.
Bibliography: p.
Includes Index.
Summary: Follows the career of a Cuban ballerina
who continues to dance despite failing eyesight.
1. Alonso, Alicia.   2. Dancers—Biography.
[1. Alonso, Alicia.   2. Dancers]   I. Title.
GV1785.A63S57   792.8'092'4   [B]   [92]   78-15410
ISBN 0-7232-6157-1

To Millicent
and to the memory of Howard

Contents

Acknowledgments

Miss Alonso approved the idea of this book when I discussed it with her in Cuba in early 1975 and expressed my wish to bring to young people the story of her life. I would like to thank her and the many others in the United States and Cuba who, in discussions and interviews, by letter or by phone, took the time to answer my questions.

Two people in particular became valuable sources of reference: Norberto Sánchez, to whom I am deeply grateful, generously shared with me his encyclopedic knowledge of Miss Alonso's career; Cuca Martínez-Hoyo made available family genealogy and her remembrances of early years.

For granting me interviews, I would like to thank Laura Alonso, Miguel Cabrera, Lucia Chase, Leon Danielian, Angela Grau, Elizabeth Gilbert, Maria Karnilova, Pauline Koner, Eugene Loring, Trude Rittmann, Pedro Simón, and Igor Youskevitch.

Others have been helpful: Dr. David Kimmelman explained medical terms; Robert Webb made editorial suggestions; Ethel Panken assisted in research; John Gruen permitted me to read typescripts of interviews related to Miss Alonso; Andra Patterson worked on the manuscript; Jane Sherman Lehac gave me advice and encouragement.

I would like to add a word of appreciation to the St. Augustine, Florida, Historical Society for sending me material placing the family in its proper historical setting.

And finally, I would like to thank the staff of the Dance Collection, New York Public Library, Lincoln Center, especially Lacy McDearmon and Reynaldo Alejandro, for their patience in making accessible vast resources of material for my research.

BEATRICE SIEGEL
New York City, 1978

Foreword

My very dear friend Alicia is best known as a great dancer, and rightly so. She is a consummate artist, one of the most magnificent dancers I have ever seen. Her dancing is truly poetry in motion, an almost spiritual experience. Naturally, Alicia's extraordinary talent is what attracted me to her in the first place. But it is not her artistry that first comes to mind when I think of her. Rather, it is her humor and exuberance, the fun we had together.

We met as teenagers in dance class and immediately became friends. From class we progressed together to Broadway shows such as *Great Lady* and *Stars in Your Eyes*. Later she joined the Ballet Theatre six months after I did. We started in the corps de ballet, then did some solos and finally got principal roles. The wonderful thing is that even though we exchanged roles, we were never jealous of each other. If anything, we had our own mutual admiration society.

Alicia was fun to be around. We shared the same dressing room and giggled most of the time. Even though she was very dedicated and worked extremely hard, she always had the knack of making me laugh. What better gift from a friend! Alicia was and is a delight.

It came as a terrible shock to all of us when we learned that this blithe spirit had such serious eye trouble. I felt so sad when she returned to Cuba for what was to be the first of several eye operations. But I also knew she had the determination to dance again, no matter what the doctors predicted . . . and when she did dance again, what an inspiration she was to us other dancers!

When we met again, after many years, I found that she acted and looked exactly the same to me, this marvelous friend who worked so hard to achieve perfection and overcame traumas that would have destroyed an ordinary person.

This chronicle of her life offers shimmers of her remarkable spirit. I am so glad I have been fortunate enough to have experienced the Alicia Alonso spirit firsthand.

NORA KAYE

Alicia Alonso

1

Growing Up in Cuba

*T*he dark-eyed little girl ran up the building's broad stone steps to a side entrance, then up a flight of narrow stairs to the second floor.

In a small dressing room she kicked off her street shoes and put on tennis shoes. Then she went down to join fifteen other young girls milling about on a large stage of the concert hall, waiting for their dancing teacher to start class.

Today thousands of children in Cuba can be found doing exercises at the barre. But in Havana, in 1931, it was a most unusual scene. That was the year that ballet had its beginning in Cuba.

And for the girl who bounded up the stairs, it was the beginning of a long struggle—against tradition, against the uncertainties of life in a foreign country, against the shattering loss of sight, against the separation from the center of the dance world at the height of her career. In that year, and on that stage, the nine-year-old girl who would become world-renowned as the great ballerina Alicia Alonso took her first ballet lessons.

The concert hall, called *Teatro Auditorium*, was housed in a building known as Pro Arte Musical, a privately endowed cultural center for Havana's middle and upper classes. The wealthy parents on Pro Arte's mailing list welcomed its classes as a way of broadening their children's cultural education. They had already found teachers for theater and music. But ballet? Who would teach it? No one in Cuba had been trained in that form of dance.

Then in 1931 Nikolai Yavorsky, a Russian with experience in ballet, arrived in Havana. He was just the man they were looking for. Charming, courteous, and educated in the ways of the Old World, he would turn their little girls into proper young ladies. He would teach them the genteel arts of poise and grace and improve their posture with exercises at the barre.

None of the wealthy parents observing the classes from the hall's orchestra seats dreamed for a moment that their daughters would become professional dancers. In those days acting and dancing professionally were considered vulgar, fit only for the lower class.

Alicia's mother signed her up for dance and drama lessons. The child had shown interest in the classes from the day they were announced. She took her first ballet lessons on the large open stage. To make it serve as a dance studio, it had been fitted with barres or hand rails along the back wall and partially down the side walls. For months Alicia danced in street clothes and tennis shoes, and sometimes in her stockinged feet. She did not mind because the other children dressed the same way. No one had ever heard of practice clothes. Nor, for that matter, had anyone ever seen a ballet or ballet costumes. It was all new. The building was new, the class was new, and the teacher Yavorsky was a newcomer to Havana.

Yet with those first lessons, Alicia knew she wanted to become a dancer. It is difficult to say what filled her with such excitement. There was no Pavlova to inspire her and there was no performing company to reveal ballet's brilliance and glamour.

For Alicia there were only an amateur teacher and a bare stage. There were, to be sure, her own talents and a will to dance. Whatever the mysterious elements are that create an artist, ballet captured that little girl and became the cornerstone of her life.

Her father and mother christened her Alicia Ernestina de la Caridad del Cobre Martínez y del Hoyo, a combination of their names, in keeping with Spanish custom. Those customs, bent to accommodate life in the Western Hemisphere, would determine not only her name but would shape her growing-up years.

Alicia came from a long line of Spanish-Cuban families going back as far as Spain's colony at St. Augustine, Florida, the first permanent European settlement in the New World. Most of her family had its origin in the north of Spain—in La Montaña or The Uplands of

Santander where rocky, snow-capped mountains tower thousands of feet above sea level.

Toward the end of the last century, Alicia's maternal grandfather came from Santander to Cuba to visit relatives. The lad became so seasick on a stormy voyage across the Atlantic Ocean that he vowed never again to make the crossing, even to return home. He settled in Havana, becoming a public official in charge of city records, and married into an old, established family.

On Alicia's father's side, the first ancestor sailed across the Atlantic from Santander nearly two hundred years ago, in 1784. In the many shifts and turns of political power at the time, Fernando de la Maza Arredondo arrived with Spain's army to occupy St. Augustine. He started out as a hospital orderly, but eventually became a rich merchant, landowner, and aide-de-camp to the governor. He married a St. Augustine woman whose ancestry went back to the Spanish conquest of Florida in the sixteenth century.

In the 1820's, when Spain was forced to cede Florida to what is now the United States, part of the Arredondo family settled in Cuba. It was from that branch that Alicia's father, Antonio Martínez de Arredondo, was descended.

There was pride of ancestry in Alicia's father and it showed itself in his conservative nature. His family from its beginnings in the New World had been part of the established order. He was born to follow rules, not to question them. In this way he was no different from most of Cuba's upper class, steeped in the Latin traditions of the time, as the blending of Spanish culture and life in the New World came to be called.

Mr. Martínez brought his conservative attitudes to the upbringing of his children—Alicia, her older sister Blanca (nicknamed Cuca), and her older brothers Antonio and Elizardo. Though he was a devoted family man, he was strict and proper even in small matters. The boys had to wear jackets at the dinner table and the girls had to be neatly dressed and combed.

Rules such as these set the tone for the children's future lives. Men, according to Latin tradition, belonged in the outside world. Alicia's brothers, therefore, could plan on college educations and careers. But women, considered frail and in need of protection, belonged in the home. They could complete secondary school, but after that they could look forward only to marriage and a family.

It seemed natural that Alicia's father would find a career in the army. Educated in the United States, he attended a private school in Florida and then a veterinary school in Georgia. By the time Alicia was born, in December 1921, he had become a military officer responsible for the care of the army's horses. Skilled in his profession, Mr. Martínez introduced into Cuba scientific breeding methods. When the army sent him abroad to do further research or to restock the supply of horses, he always took his family with him. Alicia was too young to remember the visits to the United States when her father worked in a laboratory at Walter Reed Army Hospital in Washington, D.C. She did recall other occasions when they lived briefly in Carlisle, Pennsylvania, and St. Louis, Missouri.

But wherever she lived, there was warmth and laughter in the home. It came from Alicia's mother, Ernestina del Hoyo y Lugo, a stocky, lively woman who loved the noise of her growing children. Like Alicia's father, she came from a proper middle-class family and had attended private schools. It was through her musical interests that the family belonged to Sociedad Pro Arte Musical.

Alicia's mother, a creative woman, put her talent into embroidery and lacework, an acceptable artistic outlet for women in those days. "A magician with a needle," she was called. Alicia, in later years, sitting in a dressing room putting together a headdress for a role, would remember watching her mother's busy fingers whip together an adornment from bits of fabric, beads, and ribbons. Her mother would make the first tutus—ballet skirts—in Cuba and train seamstresses in the skill.

"Everything has its bright side," was the simple adage with which Alicia's mother raised her children. "Don't cry," she often said to Alicia, drying her tears after some mishap or disappointment. "Something good will come of it, you will see."

Her mother was the center of Alicia's universe, her lifelong ally. The bond worked both ways, for her mother felt a special attachment for Alicia, her last child (a fifth child had died in its first year).

Alicia grew up with her brothers and sister in a spacious home in Vedado, a wealthy Havana suburb of tree-lined streets and palatial residences. Not only the gracious life in Vedado but the vivid natural beauty of Cuba itself was part of her landscape — the lush fertility, the drenching hot sun, the sea breaking against the shore. The streets were alive with startling colors — the purple, flaming red, and orange of tropical plants. Tall almond trees spread wide their branches, bringing welcome shade.

In the cheerful home, baby Alicia took her first steps, twirling around almost as soon as she could walk. The family called her Unga, a shortened word for *Húngaro* or Hungarian. With her olive complexion and enormous dark eyes, she seemed to them a child of gypsy grace.

She was often in motion, turning and running. Her mother found it easy to take care of her. She would put records on the phonograph, give her some scarves or a towel and say, "Here, Unga, go play." Waving the scarves or wrapping the towel over her head and letting it hang down her back as if it were long hair, Alicia would drift off into a make-believe world. She would move her body to the beat of the music, wiggle her hips, stamp her feet and experiment with her hands, shaking them, flinging them over her head, down and around. Exhausted, she would fall to the floor and stretch out to rest, but only for a moment. Then she would leap up and start again.

At other times she would sit quietly in a corner and intently rearrange paper cut-out dolls along the wall. Again she was deep in her own world. There was in her both the intense concentration as well as the energetic restlessness of the growing child.

In those early years, Alicia was bone-thin, with huge eyes dominating her face. Her little girl's body was graceful and agile. Her hair — short, straight, black — bounced over her face as she ran along the streets with the family dogs or rode the gentle mares her father carefully selected from the stables.

Her brothers and sister were also graceful and limber. With the phonograph playing, she would join them in the *son* and *danzonete*, the popular dances of the day. Later they would dance the rumba and the conga.

In those dances, Alicia absorbed the Afro-Cuban rhythms that penetrated the city from the island's interior, where the black people lived and worked. They shaped Cuba's folk music and popular dances, introducing syncopated rhythms and the use of percussion instruments. Cubans in the cities, clinging to Spanish melodies and dance, began to hear the beat of drums—the large cylindrical one called the conga and the small twin ones called bongos. They heard the maracas, hollowed gourds filled with dried seeds, and the *clavés*, two short cylindrical hardwood sticks. Musicians tapped one against the other, producing a haunting sound poetically called by a Cuban writer "the most profound emotional expression of Cuba's soul."

Alicia would say in later years, "Of course I dance the rumba and the conga. I love them. They are part of my blood."

While dancing, even the popular steps of the day, always excited Alicia, the same cannot be said about her schooling. The purpose of education, during Alicia's growing up years in Cuba, was not to stimulate a child's mind, especially a girl's mind, but to provide a smattering of knowledge. Alicia learned the basic lessons in reading, writing, and arithmetic at a private school run by nuns. Later on, at secondary school, whenever she became too busy with dancing to go to class, her parents arranged for tutors to give her lessons at home.

When she was seven, Alicia's father took the family on a ten-month trip to Spain. Before they left, they asked Alicia's grandfather what they should bring him. He answered simply that he would like the two girls to learn Spanish dancing. In that way they would bring him a piece of his homeland.

The family spent time with relatives in Santander, then took a train south to Madrid to visit the museums and fairs. From there they continued south to Jerez de la Frontera, the business destination of Alicia's father. The town was known not only for its *bodegas*, or wine cellars, for the maturing of sherry wine but also for its valued horses of mixed Arab, Spanish, and English stock.

In Jerez de la Frontera, Alicia and Cuca honored their grandfather's wish and took dancing lessons. Their first teacher, a heavyset, ungainly woman, disappeared after a few classes. Years later Alicia and Cuca realized she had been pregnant. A new teacher, young and cheerful, taught the little girls two traditional folk dances of Spain, the difficult but colorful *sevillanas* and *malagueñas*. Alicia learned the steps, but what impressed her the most, and what she always remembered, were the prideful stance of the head, the flowing, surging movements of shoulders and hips.

Adding to the enchantment of the lessons, Alicia and Cuca were taught to play the castanets, the hand-held wooden disks with which Spanish dancers click out rhythm. The castanets fascinated Alicia. She learned to loop the cord over her thumb and to beat one side against the other. So compelling was her need to master the castanets that she wore them to bed to be sure she could play them in whatever positions she held her arms and hands.

Alicia kept up with her older sister Cuca as the lessons became more complicated. They would be able to perform for their grandfather.

It seemed to Alicia that all of Spain was vibrant and gay, filled with splashing color and with crowds of celebrating, dancing people. In Jerez de la Frontera she was in the heart of gypsy country. She could hear the passionate music of flamenco, the dancers' stamping feet, the throbbing guitars, and the staccato rhythm of castanets. Haunting sounds floated out of cafés. In the market square, stalls displayed gaily colored costumes for women dancers, the tight bodices and the long, ruffled skirts, embroidered shawls, large ornate combs.

On the night of Alicia's first unforgettable visit to the theater the sky glowed with thousands of stars. She entered the old, dimly lit theater and breathed in its dusty, sweaty smells. From the moment the curtain parted, she sat transfixed. She gave herself over to fleeting dreams—dancing, theater, the starlit night. What enchantment for an imaginative little girl who until then had hardly known that the theater existed. The applause aroused her. She felt a pang of awful loss that the performance was over.

Alicia wanted to continue dancing lessons. But it was time to return to Cuba. It would be a year before she would find herself at the barre at Pro Arte Musical taking ballet lessons.

2

Learning to Dance

The dance class at Pro Arte was never long enough for Alicia. She wanted it to go on for hours. She lost all interest in the drama class and pleaded with her mother to let her drop it. The teacher objected, insisting Alicia was talented and should continue. But she won her way and took another ballet class instead.

Excitement surged through Alicia every time she turned the street corner and came upon the imposing yellow building which was only a short distance from her home. It faced the small Villalon Park with its tall shade trees, statuary, and gardens. Ornate iron lamps flanked the building's main entrance, which opened onto a lobby of marble and tile. Inside were the two thousand-seat auditorium, smaller concert halls, and administrative offices.

She walked into class eager yet apprehensive. Her teacher, Nikolai Yavorsky, was strict and cold, with an unpredictable temper. One day he was teaching his version of *The Blue Danube*. In a divertissement, a short complete dance, Alicia and another girl, Delfina, were to play with a balloon. Delfina threw the balloon to Alicia, who was to catch it on the beat to the music. Alicia missed it—the balloon floated away.

"Catch it, catch it," Yavorsky shouted.

Alicia missed it again.

In a rage, Yavorsky came over to Alicia and slammed the balloon down on her. Alicia stared at Yavorsky in disbelief, shaken but not physically hurt. Her older sister, Cuca, who by then had joined the ballet class, took Alicia's hand and said out loud, "Come, we are going home." Yavorsky followed them up to the dressing room to apologize, but Cuca demanded an apology in front of the class where the insult had taken place. Yavorsky gave it.

During class, Yavorsky sat on a folding chair in the center of the stage, his back to the parents in the auditorium. With a long stick he beat time on the floor. And in Spanish with a marked Russian accent he issued orders like military commands.

"Backs flat, straight," he ordered. "Stomachs in, stretch up, up, heads high and straight, shoulders down. No, not back, down, necks up. Relax."

In lesson after lesson, Alicia listened carefully, learning this new language.

"Come now, stretch up, up from the hips." Then he would interject by way of explanation, "Correct posture will make your backs strong and straight."

He would walk down the line of girls at the barre and with his stick tap this one on the knees—"Straight!"—and that one on the stomach—"In!"

Yavorsky took them through the demi-pliés in the five positions. "Down, one two, up three four." Tap, tap went the stick. "Come up from the legs, up, feel it in the legs."

Alicia was blessed with physical attributes that made the lessons easier for her than for many others. Her legs were strong, the muscles resilient, and she had a natural "turnout." She could also move easily with graceful coordination of movement, though dancing in tennis shoes often made her feel as if she were glued to the floor. But she felt the strain in her thighs and legs as week after week she did the exercises that were the building blocks of ballet technique.

At the end of the lesson, Alicia, reluctant to go home, often stayed on to chat with other students. Sometimes Yavorsky told them stories of famous dancers. That was when she began to like him, when he reminisced and parted the curtains to a tantalizing world.

"Ah, Pavlova," he would enthusiastically recall, "so fleet, light like a feather. Dreamlike. Floating on stage with fast light steps. An unearthly vision." He would gesture as he spoke as if he could summon her forth into that room.

"The magic of Karsavina, the favorite of Europe," he would go on. "And Nijinsky. Faultless."

Yavorsky felt an affinity for these fabled Russian dancers, for Russia was Yavorsky's native country. When the revolution in 1917 toppled the tsar, Yavorsky, then an artillery officer, fled to Yugoslavia. He taught school for several years, and then made his way to Paris. There he became part of a large colony of Russian emigré artists and professionals who eked out a living at odd jobs in restaurants, nightclubs, and cafés.

In the absence of books and magazines on the subject of dance, Alicia picked up bits and pieces of a dance education by listening to Yavorsky. She learned how Diaghilev, the great Russian impresario, in 1909 brought to Paris a fabulous group of Russian ballet dancers— Pavlova, Nijinsky, Karsavina, Bolm, Mordkin, Rubinstein. In historic performances at the Paris Opera, he moved ballet out of the tsar's Imperial Theatre, where it was an entertainment for the aristocratic élite, and presented it to the concert audiences of bourgeois Europe.

It was not only the astounding brilliance of each dancer but the revolutionary changes in choreography introduced by another Russian, Michel Fokine, that exploded in the European concert halls. Fokine liberated ballet from its fixed forms and patterns, making it easier for a broad audience to understand its meaning. In short, dramatic ballets like *Petrouchka*, he used dance to tell a story. Movement evolved out of the dramatic needs of the characters as well as out of the ballet's setting in time and place. Dancers began to move more freely, using their whole bodies in new dance techniques.

Fokine may have been influenced by the flowing style of the American dancer Isadora Duncan, who had toured Russia. But the political conditions of the period also affected him. In the first few years of the 1900's, Russia was in a political upheaval that culminated in the revolution of 1905. Fokine knew some of the radical philosophers of the day. He was sympathetic to the people's demands for a share of the economic and political privileges enjoyed by the few. When demonstrators were shot down, Fokine and Pavlova led a group of dancers in a protest against the shooting. They also became leaders of a "dancers' strike" for improved conditions and defied the tsar's orders to appear at a scheduled performance.

The Diaghilev Ballets Russes became the showcase for Fokine's significant changes in dance. And the creative genius of Diaghilev brought about a unity of the arts never before seen. In sumptuous productions, he brought together rare dancers, new choreography, avant-garde music, design, settings, costumes. Throughout Western Europe, dancers and balletomanes were stirred to pioneer in their own countries, often starting schools of ballet where none had existed.

Nikolai Yavorsky, as Alicia would learn, helped the dispersal of modern ballet from its new center in Paris. He had been on the fringe of the exploding dance scene. With some knowledge of the art, he was accepted into the studio and performing company of Ida Rubinstein, who had been a private pupil of Fokine's in Russia.

That was the tradition Yavorsky brought with him to Havana in 1930 on tour with a small opera company. He loved Cuba's tropical warmth and the surrounding sea. When his company was stranded in Mexico City, Yavorsky returned to Havana to look for work. He showed up at Pro Arte at the very time they were looking for a dance teacher.

Classes were started not only for the cultural education of Havana's élite, but also as a way to rescue Pro Arte from debt. It was 1931 and the worldwide economic depression had tumbled the price of Cuba's staple commodity, sugar. Crashing down with it were the financial empires of families who supported the cultural center. They could not even meet the bills for the newly constructed auditorium.

The committee interviewing Yavorsky for the job was not concerned that he was an amateur ballet dancer and teacher. They were drawn instead to his broad artistic interests. Yet Yavorsky introduced into the insular culture of Cuba the first school of ballet and the ballet classes soon became the highlights of Alicia's days. That did not prevent her from arriving late, however, a habit that had its beginning then. One day, late as usual, she saw a friend of hers, Leonor Albarrán, standing in the corridor.

"Run, Unga," shouted Leonor. "There's a pair of ballet shoes—I'm sure they will fit you."

Alicia did not understand what Leonor was saying, but she ran and found the girls passing around a pair of pink satin toe shoes, blocked and stiff, with gleaming satin ribbons. They were a gift to the class from a wealthy parent who had purchased them in Italy, and would belong to whomever they fit. Students were crying out in disappointment as they tried to push large feet into the shoes or stuff them with cotton for smaller feet.

Alicia took the shoes, removed the cotton and put them on. She danced out on to the stage. "Look," she shouted, "I'm on my toes."

As in the familiar tale of Cinderella's glass slipper, the shoes carried enchantment for a little girl—and Alicia became the adoring owner of the only pair of toe shoes in Cuba. That night she took them to bed with her like a precious doll.

"Ernestina, that child will never walk in a normal way," her father burst out one day to her mother, when Alicia greeted him at the door on her toes. She was on her toes all the time and when she wasn't, she carefully tucked the shoes away, trying to preserve them forever. But she wore them to shreds; even her mother could no longer darn them.

In those first months, Alicia secretly vowed to become a dancer. One word of approval would have made her day. But Yavorsky ignored her. Even when he decided to give a year-end recital, he disregarded her. Week after week he rehearsed a selected few in the grand waltz of the first act of *Sleeping Beauty*.

Alicia knew those steps. She was practicing them in a corridor one day when Yavorsky saw her. She froze in fright. "Continue," he called out. "Good, go on," he encouraged her when she tried to stop, shy at the unexpected solo. For the first time, she had captured Yavorsky's attention. He selected her to perform in the recital.

As a lady of the court, in the grand waltz of Act I of *Sleeping Beauty*, Alicia, who had just turned ten, made her debut in December 1931 on the large stage of the auditorium.

It was a special occasion for Cuba: the first performance of classical ballet by Cuban dancers in the history of the country.

For many in the audience the years fell away and they could recall a memorable event thirteen years before. At Havana's *Teatro Nacional* (now *Teatro García Lorca*) Anna Pavlova and her company had presented a shortened version of *Sleeping Beauty*. To Pavlova's Princess Aurora, Alexander Volinine danced the role of the prince.

The enthusiasm for his students' brief recital encouraged Yavorsky to plan a full version of *Sleeping Beauty* for the end of 1932. In that production Alicia danced her first solo role. She was the Bluebird in Act III, costumed all in feathers and wearing a beaked helmet. Fluttering long thin arms in light airy movements, she soared in flight across the large stage, paying homage to the marriage of Princess Aurora and the prince. It was a triumphant day for Alicia. She received her first public notice in a glowing tribute by Yavorsky.

"Among my pupils," he said, "are many who are doing three years' work in one. This ballet is a result of sixteen months of collective lessons. Among my top pupils are Delfina Pérez Gurri and Alicia Martínez."

In the next two years Alicia danced solo roles in many ballets, choreographed by Yavorsky or staged by him after the choreography of Fokine and Petipa. They included *El Circo (La Bailarina de la Cuerda Floja)*, *Polka Coquette*, a Raff-Yavorsky number, and *Tartaritos*, after Fokine's *Prince Igor* to Borodin's music.

The ballet school was so successful that it was moved to its own quarters on the fourth floor. A long narrow room, with a bank of windows overlooking Villalon Park, had been properly outfitted with barres and mirrors. In one corner the pianist Luis Borbolla played for advanced students. Off the studio were dressing rooms—all students now had practice clothes—and an anteroom for parents.

Alicia spent all her free time in the studio. That was the only place she wanted to be. She rushed home from school, threw down her books, grabbed her practice clothes, and hurried off to Pro Arte. She took class every day, including Yavorsky's private sessions at which she demonstrated difficult exercises and steps for beginners.

Her mother often had to send someone to fetch her at the end of the day. "That's enough," the maid Maria would call out, coaxing Alicia from the studio. "Let's go home. You have to have dinner and study."

Her parents worried over her new life.

"What does she do there all day?" her father complained. Alicia's enthusiasm for ballet was alien to him. He was an athlete and a fanatic about good health. But ballet? In his view, it was frivolous, absurd to spend all one's time at a dance studio! But it made Alicia happy so he indulged her in the pastime.

Alicia's mother watched the gay, mischievous child grow into a private girl. Proud of Alicia's talent, she nevertheless felt concern over her growing estrangement from old friends. There were few left.

"Go to the party," Ernestina would plead with Alicia when she received an invitation. Alicia never argued with her mother. She kept quiet. But when party time came around, she ran instead to the dance studio.

She gave up games and sports, even her favorite—roller skating. In a bad fall she had bruised her legs and missed dance class. She gave away her skates. Horseback riding strained muscles that made it difficult to dance. She gave up horseback riding.

She wanted only to dance. It engaged her completely, her bright young mind, her energy, and her need to express herself. It awakened her in unexpected ways like the dance exercises that stretched her body into a different and unexpected shape. Her life had once been fixed, the future mapped. But dancing challenged these old patterns, filling her with new excitement.

She was turning into a lovely young girl. She had enormous eyes and clearly defined features that would never blur on stage. Her hair, now thick and long, was caught back in a ribbon or hung down her back as she had once dreamed. She was petite, small-boned with a tiny waist, sloping shoulders, and a strong neck. Her feet were beautiful, small with taut arches. The arms were rounded and soft. The legs created miracles when she extended one upward to some incredible height.

Alicia thrilled Yavorsky with her dancing. She would be a great ballerina, he thought, but he could train her just so far. Though he had grown as a teacher, his knowledge of ballet technique was limited and in some ways poor. But Alicia did learn from Yavorsky how to appreciate music, how to dance to its phrasing and melody so that she could give feeling to the movements of her arms and body.

Alicia was ready for something new when Laura Rayneri de Alonso became president of Sociedad Pro Arte Musical in 1934. Concert pianist, music teacher and society woman, she was committed to expanding Cuba's cultural life. She had behind her the prestige of an old family of architects who had designed Havana's *Teatro Tacón*.

Laura Rayneri dedicated her best efforts to the ballet school. She saw in it an opportunity to develop native talent as well as to educate audiences to an appreciation of classical dance. In her fourteen years of leadership Pro Arte Musical would open its doors to a much wider public. Seats were offered to nonmembers. Tickets were priced lower for students. And ballet became part of the schedule, no longer sandwiched between visiting opera stars. Resulting from her dedication were performances at Pro Arte by top dance companies and soloists.

Laura Rayneri's youngest son, Alberto Alonso, encouraged by his mother, had joined the ballet class in 1933. Word had spread that ballet was good for athletes, that it strengthened the muscles. Fortified by this new mystique, a few daring young men had begun ballet lessons. Alberto Alonso, striking-looking, educated in private schools in the United States, showed talent and soon became a serious student.

With young men enrolled, Yavorsky had new opportunities for programing. Up to then girls had danced male roles. For the 1935 season, he planned to stage the ballet *Coppélia* with Alicia in the lead as Swanilda and Alberto as her partner in the role of Franz.

The ballet, set to the music of Delibes, tells the gay, comic story of two young people in love who get mixed up with a mechanical doll and an old doll-maker. The ballet ends with the marriage of Swanilda and Franz and a joyous pas de deux in a happy village festival.

Though Yavorsky's version was not the expanded ballet known today, it was Alicia's first full-length role. Working on it, she began developing habits that would remain with her a lifetime. She not only practiced the role's steps but she tried to absorb its special texture. Who was Swanilda? What was her background? Alicia was too young to grasp fully the ballet's intracacies. But she had an opportunity to display her acting ability in scenes of pantomime, that special art that develops the action of a story by the use of expressive gestures.

In the nervous, noisy backstage activity on the day of the performance, only Alicia's eyes showed her excitement. She felt no stage fright—only the thrill of performing. She had been taking lessons on that same stage for years and she thought of it as a second home. Intent on her role, Alicia put on her stage makeup, her costume and ballet shoes, and then rehearsed a few particularly demanding steps. With each motion, she put more of herself into the part.

It was a gala evening that spring in 1935 when Pro Arte presented its first full-length ballet. The single performance was open only to its members. The orchestra, under the direction of composer-conductor Amadeo Roldán, played the introduction. And then, in a bright, thrilling entrance, thirteen-year-old Alicia came onstage as a gay, exuberant village girl in a spirited dance. She was a delight, projecting the ballet's lighthearted charm over the footlights to the audience.

At the end of the evening, the hall shook with applause for Alicia Martínez and Alberto Alonso as well as for Yavorsky's efforts.

Joining in the ovation was an attractive young man, Fernando Alonso, the older of Laura Rayneri's two sons. He was home on holiday from business school in the United States.

3

A Bold Decision

*A*licia and Fernando had known each other for a long time. Years back she was the skinny little girl who had opened the door when he came to pick up her brother Antonio on the way to a party. She was on her toes even then, in her first pair of toe shoes, energetically dancing around him as if, like Coppélia, she was a wound-up toy doll.

"My God," Fernando thought, "she's crazy about dancing. Someday she will be a great ballerina."

In recent years Fernando had been away at school in North Carolina. He knew little of the unfolding ballet scene in Havana and of its lead dancer. But that evening in 1935, his enthusiasm for *Coppélia* was matched only by his enthusiasm for Alicia. For Alicia, on the threshold of young womanhood, Fernando was her first love, as important as her dancing.

When Fernando decided he too would study ballet, it brought the two young people together day after day. Alicia was his teacher and his partner. She kept his spirits up with her enthusiasm as he worked at age nineteen to turn his body into that of a dancer.

Alicia could share with Fernando her excitement, her tirelessness. Yet her own knowledge of dance history and her opportunity to learn and grow were limited.

She had been too young to appreciate the performance of the American ballet dancer Ruth Page at Pro Arte in the spring of 1932. It had been a rare event, for most performers touring in Havana were instrumentalists and opera stars. Stored in Alicia's memory were images of the outstanding ones—Josef Hoffman, Vladimir Horowitz, Ezio Pinza, Lotte Lehman.

When she learned that a Spanish dancer called La Argentina (Antonia Mercé) was going to perform at Pro Arte in 1935, Alicia attended rehearsals. She saw a woman come out on stage wrapped in bulky woolen leg warmers. Good God, thought Alicia, how can she dance! She looks as if she was in an automobile accident.

That afternoon Alicia had to audition for La Argentina, who was choosing dancers for a small company in Spain. Alicia danced a number created by Yavorsky. It was so lengthy, she forgot it in the middle of her performance. When she started to dance it again La Argentina laughed at the young serious girl and said to her, "You must work very hard."

That evening Alicia saw La Argentina come out on stage in a colorful costume with a tight bodice and flaring skirt—and smile at the audience. Suddenly audience, theater, friends fell away. The smile illuminated the hall and captured the heart of little Alicia. She sat spellbound. Onstage, she saw only La Argentina who, with tapping heels, flowing movements of torso and arms and subtle playing of castanets, presented the proud, passionate dances of the Spanish people.

After the performance, Alicia went backstage with dozens of other smitten dance lovers to get La Argentina's autograph.

"You. That one with the big eyes and the big smile. You," La Argentina called out to Alicia. "I remember you. Come here." La Argentina signed Alicia's program.

Like Pavlova, who inspired a young generation, La Argentina awakened Alicia to the scope and full artistry of dance. Alicia thought back to her first lessons in Spain and how far she had developed. But the art of dance—its splendor, its gleam—how would she learn that? Who would teach it to her? How would she improve?

She was aroused to new possibilities when Yavorsky took Alberto Alonso and Delfina Pérez Gurri to Paris to audition for the prestigious Ballet Russe de Monte Carlo. Yavorsky's friend, Vasili de Basil, with René Blum, had formed the Ballet Russe from the nucleus of the Diaghilev organization after the great impresario's death in 1929. Both Alberto and Delfina were accepted into the corps de ballet, a coup for any teacher. Delfina remained with the company only a short time, but Alberto developed into a notable caractère dancer.

Alicia would see for herself what this notable company was like, for in September 1935 announcements appeared in the Havana press heralding the coming of the Ballet Russe de Monte Carlo. It was a triumph for Laura Rayneri—the first major dance company to appear since Pavlova and her group in 1918.

Alicia and the other Pro Arte students pored over the stories and pictures in the press. They soon would see the glorious prima ballerina Alexandra Danilova and the choreographer-dancer Leonide Massine. But more intriguing were the three "baby ballerinas," prodigies of the Russian emigré dance world. There was Tamara Toumanova, discovered at age seven by Pavlova, guest artist with the Paris Opera Company at age ten, and a sensation at thirteen. And blond Irina Baronova and her multiple fouettés, that unsupported turn in which the dancer stands on one leg and whips herself around with the other. And the light ethereal Tatiana Riabouchinska, who could cross the stage in magic leaps.

It was a fashionable gathering of Havana's socialites that opening night in March 1936, in the auditorium of Pro Arte Musical. The young ballet dancers of Pro Arte had eyes only for the stage. They watched Toumanova in *Prince Igor*, Massine in *Three-Cornered Hat*, and Baronova in *The Marriage of Aurora*. The next day they went again to see the ballerinas in *Les Sylphides, Blue Danube,* and *Les Presages*.

Though Alicia had performed in Yavorsky's versions of some of the ballets, these were unfamiliar. She saw a range of technique that she never knew existed. And she discovered again what she realized from watching La Argentina, that the world of dance was infinite and gripping. On the heels of it came another realization—to learn to dance she would have to leave Havana.

Among the members of the corps of the Ballet Russe de Monte Carlo as it left Havana to continue its tour was Alberto Alonso. He and Delfina Pérez Gurri had broken with the tradition of their class. Alicia began to think about her own future.

At fifteen she had reached the top at Pro Arte and she was the ballet star of Havana. To develop further she would have to leave for New York, in her mind the center of the dance world.

She had many reasons for her decision. In the five years of studying with Yavorsky, she had been repeating the same routines. There was no one to stretch her mind, to help her progress. The lack of a performing company limited her to three or four appearances a year.

She shared her dreams with Fernando. They talked long hours while they rehearsed Yavorsky's version of *Claro de la Luna (Claire de La Lune)*, the first ballet they would do together. They discussed love, marriage, careers, as they strolled through the cobbled dusty plazas of old Havana and sat on rocks rimming the sea.

Something else added to Alicia's restlessness, though it was only at the edge of her consciousness. Havana had been a center of political turmoil long before her birth. The city was continuously wracked by strikes, uprisings, and protests against U.S. domination.

In their wake came bloody suppression. At the end of 1930, a few months before Yavorsky started ballet classes for the wealthy children of Vedado, the dictator Gerardo Machado declared martial law, closed the University of Havana, and ended civil liberties. In 1933, after government troops had cut down hundreds of people, Machado was overthrown—only to be replaced by a succession of presidents under the strong arm of Fulgencio Batista, a former army sergeant who eventually became dictator himself.

But Havana was a strange city, cleaved into sections, separate and apart, each invisible to the other.

Alicia was young and secluded in her upper-class suburb, for the most part impervious to these years of turmoil. She knew nothing of the hovels of the poor or of their mysterious magic of survival that defied hunger and despair. She never saw students pour out of the University of Havana and wind down the streets to join the unemployed before the presidential palace, demanding better lives.

But sometimes the violence shattered the quiet of the tree-lined streets of Vedado, jolting Alicia and her family out of their passivity. Alicia would burst into her home and cry out, "Why are they killing students and workers when they are demanding their rights? Why . . . why . . . why?"

Once, in the innocence of her mind, she came up with a panacea for Cuba's ills. "Why don't they plant fruit trees so that people will have food?" she wanted to know.

Her father, though he had no part in the army's repressions, did not answer her questions. Often he showed his sympathies for the poor.

He would relate at dinner how he had given a worker a lift or had taken a peasant to the hospital.

Alicia did not understand the political upheaval. Yet the militant protests year after year charged the atmosphere with demands for change. And the time arrived when Alicia herself had to become, in her way, a rebel though she would never call herself that. She had to take a position against the traditions her father held so dear. Tied to a bygone era, he could not understand her simple needs. He viewed performing on the stage as a profession fit only for prostitutes.

When Alicia decided she wanted to leave Havana, she turned to her mother, who had long recognized her daughter's need for a different life. She had nurtured Alicia's independence and did not stand in the way of her wish to go to New York. Looking at her with great love and concern, she cautioned her about becoming a dancer. "There is danger," she said to Alicia, "because people will talk. They will say you are lighthearted and frivolous if you perform on the stage. Be sure this is what you want to do—and be careful."

Throughout early 1937, while Alicia and Fernando discussed their plans, she was rehearsing for Yavorsky's most ambitious project, his version of *Swan Lake*. In this three-act ballet, Alicia would dance the role of Odette-Odile. Emile Laurens, a soloist with de Basil's Ballet Russe, was brought in to partner her. Alicia, tireless in rehearsals, ignored blistered feet, stretched tendons, and aching muscles. No matter how well she did, she drove herself to do better.

The presentation of *Swan Lake* in May 1937 was a gala for the members of Pro Arte Musical. Amadeo Roldán led the fifty-two-piece Philharmonic Orchestra. Sets were designed by the artist Manolo Roig, and the luxurious costumes were made by a couturier at the exclusive department store, Fin de Siglo.

The critics were lavish in their praise. One reviewer called Alicia a "child prodigy" and exclaimed in pride over her "winged feet," "her charm," her sense of "music, acting." Above all, one reviewer commented, there was the discipline it required for Alicia to tame "her vivacious spirit for the taxing art."

But after one performance, it was over. It was time to leave for New York. Fernando was already there and had found a job. Alicia's mother helped her get ready for her departure. At last, chaperoned by the wife of Cuba's general consul in New York, Mrs. Natalia Suárez, Alicia boarded a ship for New York.

At fifteen, the age of young womanhood in Cuba, she was on a vessel sailing north. During the few days of the trip, conflicting feelings washed over her. Her confidence would turn to panic, or elation would give way to fear. Most of the time, though, she held on to her calm, remembering this was her decision and that she longed for a more challenging life.

Alicia's mother, Ernestina del Hoyo y Lugo

Alicia's father, Antonio Martínez de Arredondo

As a teenager with sister Cuca (opposite page)

Alicia at eleven

At age 10 in first ballet costume for *Sleeping Beauty* (opposite page)

Nikolai Yavorsky, Alicia's first ballet teacher

Alicia at thirteen with Alberto Alonso in *Coppélia* (opposite page)

Sociedad Pro Arte Musical; on the right are present headquarters of
Ballet Nacional de Cuba

4

Apprenticeship in New York

$\mathcal{F}$ernando was at the New York pier waiting for Alicia. With her first steps, she stretched her neck upward past the tall buildings, looking for the sky. For a moment she felt closed in. The streets were so narrow and there were no trees. She clung to Fernando.

Alicia and Fernando were married soon after her arrival. They started housekeeping in a large room on Manhattan's West Side, rented from a Cuban woman who shared her apartment to make ends meet. That Fernando had a job did not strike them as remarkable. Filled with innocence, and strangers to the city, they did not sense the tensions of the times. They were hardly aware that in 1937 the United States was still digging itself out of the worst economic depression in its history, though by then its cutting edge had been blunted by a vast program of federally funded projects. Dancers, writers, composers, artists, architects, designers—often as hungry as the unemployed laborer—were put to work. They used their art to reveal the American condition. They explored it on canvas ("Bread Line" by Reginald Marsh), in books (*The Grapes of Wrath* by John Steinbeck), on film, on stage, and in photographs.

Dance, too, was part of this revolution in the arts. To Alicia's surprise, the city to which she had so hopefully adventured was not a center of ballet but a center of new creative techniques called modern or contemporary dance. Even the names were new: Hanya Holm, Helen Tamiris, Martha Graham, Anna Sokolow, Doris Humphrey, Charles Weidman, Pauline Koner.

Young people had turned against ballet. They said its movements were decorative and meaningless, that its stodgy legends of enchanted princes had no relationship to the conditions of modern life. What did ballet have to do with haunting realities like hunger and the homelessness of millions? Thus Tamiris created a dance called "Momentum: Prelude—Unemployed." Anna Sokolow did "Strange American Funeral." Reviewers found these dances "bold, forceful, brilliant." They were as elemental as the earth from which they seemed to spring.

Artists of the Depression years responded to another tragedy unfolding across the ocean, the Spanish Civil War. In the dance columns in early 1938, there was a unique entry: "Dance Program for Spanish Democracy." One of the participating groups was the "Ballet Caravan, Lincoln Kirstein, Director." Among the performers were Eugene Loring, Lew Christensen, Erick Hawkins, Marie-Jeanne. One day Alicia would meet these dancers and piece it all together.

It was an awesome city to which Alicia had come. The emotionally charged artistic atmosphere of the Depression years was alien to her. She not only did not understand it, it did not address itself to her needs. She was young, full of romance and life was wonderful.

She had been part of the birth of ballet in Cuba and she had arrived in New York when American ballet companies were struggling to take shape. There were great teachers, however, and she would find them. For the dream of learning fully the complex technique of ballet was central to her life.

Before she could move in that direction, she and Fernando had to buy a crib for the baby that was on its way. It did not stop them from converting their large room into a studio. They laughed through many evenings of make-believe, when she danced the role of a prima ballerina to his danseur noble in the classics or in their own pas de deux.

Suddenly the world of professional dance opened to them. Fernando was accepted into the corps of the Mordkin Ballet Company for its 1937–38 tour. They were no longer in a make-believe world but could now share the hard facts of ballet life that Fernando brought home to Alicia each day.

At the head of the company was Mikhail Mordkin, a giant of the ballet world at that time. He had been premier danseur for eleven years with the Imperial Moscow Ballet and was tapped by Diaghilev for his 1909 Paris concert. In 1910 Pavlova and Mordkin appeared in *Coppélia* at the New York Metropolitan Opera House. It was the beginning of American ballet as we know it today.

Mordkin separated from Pavlova and, in 1924, settled in New York where he established his own school and a short-lived performing company. In 1937, with the help of Lucia Chase, a talented dancer and a young woman of independent wealth, he put together another company. It was there that Fernando started his American career as a dancer. It also marked the beginning of Alicia's American dance education. She came to know the prima ballerina Lucia Chase, lead danseur Leon Varkas, and soloists Karen Conrad and Nina Stroganova.

Alicia rehearsed with Fernando the repertory of four numbers the Mordkin company was preparing at its Carnegie Hall studio. They included *Giselle,* in which Fernando as a corps member was doing the peasant dance in Act I. That was her introduction to the great romantic ballet in which Alicia would later be hailed as one of the great Giselles of all time.

But now Alicia was getting restless, eager to resume ballet lessons. She searched around her neighborhood for a class and found one nearby. A few weeks after the birth of baby Laura, in the spring of 1938, she left the infant in the care of her neighbor and made her way to Rutgers Church on West Seventy-third Street. In the basement of the church, ballet classes were given as part of an adult recreation program sponsored by the Depression-born Public Works Administration. Each lesson cost 25 cents.

The teacher, Enrico Zanfretta, was then in his mid-seventies. He had had his own school for years but during the Depression and the low ebb of ballet he had lost his following. Rescued from near-poverty by the Federal Dance Project, he again could put to use his enormous skills.

Zanfretta taught without music. He did not believe in it, which was typical of dance education in his native Italy. Like his famous countryman, the dancer and pedagogue Enrico Cecchetti, Zanfretta believed that discipline, hard work, and the day-to-day repetition of correct exercises were the secret to a dancer's development.

Sitting on a chair in the center of the room, Zanfretta used his cane to tap out the beat. Occasionally he would gently tap a student on the knee or foot to call attention to an incorrect movement. An advanced student assisted him.

In her first few classes Alicia was painfully shy. She understood only a few words of English and found it difficult to follow Zanfretta's instructions. She learned by observing rather than by listening. "I felt as if I had eyes all over my head," she would put it later.

After a while the warmth and friendliness of the other young people in class made her feel more comfortable. They found Alicia endearing, with her gentle, husky voice and broad smile. She seemed to them a child, only sixteen, and much too young to be a mother. They worried over her. They wondered if she should have returned to ballet so soon after the birth of a baby. But they were reassured about her health by the simple show of her energy.

Even in those early weeks, it was clear that Alicia was a gifted dancer. One student, Leon Danielian, remembers how awed he was by Alicia's natural abilities, her extension and turnout. Another student, Maria Karnilova, thought how hard she and others would have to work to accomplish the technical feats that came so easily to Alicia. "She's a born dancer," the young Maria would say later, admiring Alicia's "turnout, flexible back and marvelously flexible arms." But Alicia began to feel secure about her evolving ballet technique only as she practiced in class and at home the exercises she learned from Zanfretta. And what she essentially was learning were the difficult quick beats—the batterie. She absorbed into her technique the quick, clean, rapid footwork that would always mark her style and which gave her dancing such lightness.

Her sense of security also came from Fernando, whose knowledge of English brought order to the chaotic world outside her door. He had already made the first successful forays into the New York dance world. There had been the all-too-brief months with the Mordkin Ballet Company. And in the summer of 1938 he found a job in a musical called *Three Waltzes* to be produced in the municipal stadium at Long Island's Jones Beach.

"Over the water and under the stars," read the advertisements for the enormous arena with a stage floating on water. There musicals, operettas, and other light entertainment were produced each night for the enjoyment of capacity crowds of ten thousand or more people.

Alicia and Laurita, as the baby was affectionately called, often accompanied Fernando to rehearsals. On the bridge that led from the arena to the stage, Alicia practiced the dance routines with Fernando. One day dance director Marjorie Fielding saw her and called out to Alicia, "You're wonderful, a great dancer. I'd love you to give my daughter Lorie lessons. Do you want to teach a small group?"

Miss Fielding formed a class of the children of Jones Beach performers. Lorie never forgot her first dance teacher—"beautiful, slender, dark Alicia and her incredible extensions."

Both Miss Fielding and her husband, co-director Charles Barnes, saw such promise in Alicia that Miss Fielding added a special dance number for her to *Three Waltzes*.

Dressed in a long white gown of floating chiffon, her dark hair coiffed close to her head and caught back in a chignon, an elegant Alicia Alonso appeared on stage with two men as partners. They whirled her through a complicated waltz with soaring lifts and turns.

Thus Alicia made her debut on the American stage—at Jones Beach. It was hardly the one she had dreamed of but it was dancing and it was a job. Determined to support themselves with only emergency help from their families, Alicia and Fernando went where the jobs were. Jones Beach paid for ballet lessons and put them in a position to hear theater news and especially gossip about auditions for new plays.

After the summer season, Alicia and Fernando were accepted into the chorus of a new Broadway operetta called *Great Lady*, with music by Frederick Loewe and choreography by William Dollar. Signed up as lead dancers were André Eglevsky, Annabelle Lyon, and Leda Anchutina. With the new names and new faces Alicia was again adding to her dance education, learning about the expert training and professional experience of star dancers. Eglevsky, for example, had studied with those wonderful Russian emigré dance teachers she had always heard about, including Egorova, Kshessinska, and Volinine, who partnered Pavlova when she danced in Cuba.

For much of a year, Alicia was caught up in the costly, dazzling world of musical productions. The lavish expenditure of money on elaborate costumes, sets, and new technical devices such as revolving stages, amazed her. Traveling with the company on its pre-Broadway tryouts in Philadelphia, New Haven, and Boston, she watched the production being brought to life. With her lively curiosity she found interest even in dreary trains and hotel rooms. Only her lack of English worried her. When people addressed her, her large eyes would register her fright and confusion, and call forth from directors, crew, secretaries, and stars a few kind, reassuring words.

Despite its sophisticated new devices and talent, *Great Lady* opened to poor reviews in New York. Only the dancing received praise. The critics called the ballet stunning, the highlight of the show. Arthur Pollack, in the *Brooklyn Eagle,* found the second act pas de sept "altogether beguiling." Brooks Atkinson in the *New York Times* praised the lovely ballet and its choreographer. These were perceptive comments, for the chorus glittered with brilliant but yet unknown talent. In addition to Alicia and Fernando, there were Nora Kaye, Jerome Robbins, and Paul Godkin, young people at the beginning of their careers, taking any job until classical ballet would come of age in New York.

A couple of months after *Great Lady* closed, Alicia and Fernando were accepted into the chorus of another Broadway play, this one more successful. It was an extravaganza called *Stars in Your Eyes,* directed by Joshua Logan with Ethel Merman and Jimmy Durante in the leads. The dancing star was Tamara Toumanova, the "baby" ballerina Alicia had seen perform in Havana three years before with the Ballet Russe de Monte Carlo. Alicia again observed the strong technique of the glamorous Toumanova. But she began to sort out what to do and what not to do, taking the first steps toward shaping her own style.

In spite of the glamour and immediate excitement of Broadway theater, Alicia was never tempted to leave the slow, grinding study of classical ballet. Indeed, her Broadway experience strengthened her conviction that she was pointed in the right direction. She and Fernando, she learned, were part of a steady stream of talented people from faraway towns and villages making New York a rich resource for an expanding dance world. A scholarship at the School of American Ballet put her in touch with the burgeoning dance movement, and out of the school would come Alicia's first professional ballet experience in the United States.

The moving spirit behind the school was Lincoln Kirstein, whose passion for ballet committed him to a lifelong career of fostering it in the United States. Kirstein had seen the Diaghilev company in Europe in the 1920's. It aroused in him the same ballet-madness that inspired so many others to become pioneers in their own countries. Kirstein recognized the lack of a ballet tradition in the United States. But he saw no reason why he could not found on American soil a ballet school and a performing company that would use classical ballet techniques shaped to the native attributes and spirit of the American dancer. He hoped that choreographic talent would develop that would create dances responsive to the American scene.

Kirstein—using his own personal wealth and supported for a while by banker and art patron Edward M. M. Warburg—succeeded in making a reality out of his basic convictions.

To set up a ballet school he brought over from Europe in 1933 a distinguished young choreographer named George Balanchine who had been trained in the Russian Imperial schools and had served as ballet master with the Diaghilev company. With Kirstein behind him, Balanchine and a fellow Russian emigré named Vladimir Dimitriew founded the School of American Ballet.

Alicia, in her classes at the school, the first of its kind in the United States, had the advantage of excellent classwork and the strict discipline imposed by a faculty trained, for the most part, in the Russian schools of dance. Balanchine gave classes as did Pierre Vladimiroff, Pavlova's last partner, and the English-born Muriel Stuart, a protégé of Pavlova. The equally brilliant teachers Anatole Vilzak and Anatole Oboukhoff would later join the faculty.

The school broadened the dimensions of talented young students. Under the extraordinary Balanchine, many reached levels of balance, precision, speed, and lightness they had never hoped to achieve. The school also inspired talented dancers to turn to choreography. And it fostered in 1934 a new performing group called the American Ballet Company, which would become the resident company of the Metropolitan Opera House for a few years, go out of existence in 1939, then reemerge in 1948 as the New York City Ballet.

Ballet Caravan, an experimental touring company and dance laboratory for American genre dancing, grew out of both the school and the company. The year was 1936 and the Depression had created an atmosphere of defeat and despair. Kirstein, like many others, felt called upon to revive America's fighting spirit. He would do it by encouraging the development of ballet that would deal with American themes and would reflect the country's history and customs.

At first there was an excess of zeal in Kirstein's determination to found an American ballet company. Dancers had to prove American citizenship. Even Balanchine, Dimitriew, and other European-born staff members had to take out citizenship papers. This restriction soon lapsed when it was criticized as unnecessary. But the forward thrust of Americanism continued. Advertisements called Ballet Caravan an American company with a repertory of new ballets by Americans.

Like a magician pulling a rabbit out of a hat, Kirstein made it happen. From its first New England tour in 1936, Ballet Caravan was a success. Talented young choreographers, fulfilling Kirstein's mandate, created ballets on American themes to music by American composers with costumes and designs by American artists.

Alicia and Fernando joined the company (now called American Ballet Caravan) in 1939 for its second cross-country tour. But before they could join the tour, they had to make some plan for the care of their baby daughter, Laura, now a year and a half old. Alicia had often taken Laura to class and to rehearsals with her or had left her with baby-sitters and friends. But for the tour, she and Fernando needed a long-range plan, one that would ease their minds. They decided to ask the two sets of grandparents in Havana to take care of Laura. As it turned out, Laura thrived in Havana and the grandparents adored having her. The arrangement lasted for many years and made it possible for Alicia to pursue her career.

At the studios of the School of American Ballet on East Fifty-ninth Street, Alicia and Fernando took part in their first rehearsals. The dancers in the company had had years of association with Balanchine: the beautiful prima ballerina Marie-Jeanne; soloist Gisella Caccialanza, who had trained under Cecchetti in Italy; also the soloist Ruby Asquith, a product of the school; ballet master Lew Christensen, and lead dancers Harold Christensen, Todd Bolender, Michael Kidd, Fred Danieli, and Eugene Loring, who was on temporary leave.

In the new repertory created for American Ballet Caravan, Alicia began to rehearse ballets that were different in subject, style, spirit, and in movement from anything she had known. Gone from them was the romance of sleeping princesses and enchanted swans. Gone were the divertissements to music of Chopin or Borodin. Alicia found herself learning a ballet called *Filling Station,* about a gas station attendant, choreographed by Lew Christensen, based on a book by Lincoln Kirstein, with music by Virgil Thomson, and costumes by Paul Cadmus. There was *Billy the Kid,* created by Eugene Loring to music by Aaron Copland. There were Loring's *City Portrait,* Christensen's *Charade – or the Debutante,* and William Dollar's *Air and Variations.*

Alicia found it especially difficult to relate to modern American music. In Copland's score for *Billy the Kid,* she could not follow the unfamiliar melody and rhythm. Instead she learned to count—to go onstage and dance to her own system of timing.

Not only was the repertory difficult and unfamiliar but the enthusiastic young Americans in the troupe had worked together for many years and enjoyed a close working relationship. Often in their familiarity they spoke a rapid English that skipped past Alicia with strange words that sounded like modern American music with its atonality. Her natural shyness turned into reserve and she sometimes appeared distant. Confusing her at times was the American way of doing things. She described one American custom to friends back home: In the United States, she explained, when a woman marries, she takes her husband's name, whereas in Cuba a married woman retains her maiden name. "It was Mrs. Alonso do this, Mrs. Alonso do that," she said. "So now I am Alicia Alonso and no longer Alicia Martínez."

But Alicia had her own distinctive flair. The pianist for the company, Trude Rittmann, recalled Alicia's first rehearsal. When the petite young dancer took class, the pianist overheard Ruby Asquith whisper to Gisella Caccialanza, "Did you see that arabesque?" It was sensational.

The company included some twenty dancers, a stagehand, and two pianists. With little money for comforts, the company had to be self-sufficient in every way. A caravan is exactly what it was, although a small one—a bus for members of the company and a truck for costumes, scenery, lighting equipment, and stage props. The stagehand relied on local help and other members of the company to set up a ballet.

Managing agent Frances Hawkins had booked the company for

thirty-five performances across the country—on college campuses, in civic auditoriums, and concert halls. Sometimes the group performed before fewer than a dozen people.

It was an exhausting trek of one-night stands—from the Northeast down to the South, then up to the Midwest, out to the Pacific Coast and into the Canadian Northwest, then down again into California. Like the others, Alicia tried to rest and even to sleep in the lurching bus or occasional train. Through dusty windows she could see endless open stretches of land or a blur of villages and towns.

One incident etched the Canadian Northwest on her mind. On a slow, monotonous train ride from Seattle to Vancouver, they had halted outside a small town for a fifteen-minute stopover. While everyone else rushed into the station to buy sandwiches, Alicia, Fernando, and the Cuban-born assistant pianist, Pablo Miguel, hurried into town for a bowl of hot soup. Just as they returned, they saw the train pulling out, taking not only their luggage but possibly their careers as well.

They hastened over to the stationmaster. "Get the taxi," he shouted at them. There was only one in town. "Follow the train," he advised. He would wire ahead for the train to stop at a certain pass. For a tense hour and a half, the taxi sped along an upper road parallel to the tracks below, keeping the train in view all the time. At the designated pass, the three young people happily rejoined the company.

For Alicia the ten-week tour was an intensive learning experience. She lived and breathed dance as if she had been placed in a greenhouse and at last could put down her first roots. She watched, listened, learned, rehearsed, then danced her small roles at each performance.

Typical of its obscure auspices and program was an evening early in the tour when the company was presented by the "Lecture Entertainment Course of the Women's College at the University of North Carolina." Alicia danced in the ensemble of *Air and Variations,* as a dance-hall girl in *Billy the Kid,* and as a passer-by in *City Portrait.*

By the end of December, when the company returned to New York, Alicia was a soloist. She danced the roles of the mother and the Mexican sweetheart in *Billy the Kid,* with Michael Kidd as Billy. She also danced part of a solo in Dollar's *Promenade* and was one of the Graces in the variation called *Three Graces with Satyr.*

American Ballet Caravan had fulfilled Kirstein's early dream. The company brought to American audiences ballets that sprang from the American experience. *New York Times* critic John Martin caught the message. He lauded *Billy the Kid*, writing: "Loring has managed by the simplest means imaginable to capture the atmosphere of the land and the peoples of the Old West. . . ." *Billy the Kid* has since become the first American ballet classic.

Alicia was hardly aware of how much she had absorbed of the American idiom. But when the press called Ballet Caravan an "authentic American ballet company" with a troupe of "fresh young American dancers," Alicia felt it an apt description of herself. She was beginning to feel like an American dancer.

5

Ballet Theatre

*A*fter the tour Alicia and Fernando returned to Havana for a visit with their families. They would be there to celebrate Laurita's second birthday and to dance the lead roles in the first Cuban ballet to be produced.

Changes had taken place at Pro Arte's ballet school. Yavorsky had been succeeded by George Milenoff who, like Yavorsky, was a Russian emigré who had toured Latin America with a small opera company. Milenoff was choreographing a ballet called *Dioné*, written by Eduardo Sánchez de Fuentes, a composer of symphonic works and a writer on Cuban music. Other Cuban ballets had been composed, notably Amadeo Roldán's *La Rebambaramba*, but none had ever been produced.

In two scenes, with imaginative divertissements, *Dioné* tells about the love between a young girl and a handsome prince. Performing the lead roles in it, Alicia and Fernando would set a trend that would last for decades. They would always return to Cuba to dance, enriching it with their improved balletic skills. And the American dancer Newcomb Rice of Ballet Caravan, dancing with them in *Dioné*, would be one of many ballet friends whom Alicia and Fernando would invite to dance in Cuba. Though *Dioné* was not successful as a ballet, it was another seed planted for the growth of Cuban dance.

A few days after the performance, Alicia and Fernando returned to New York where they learned that auditions were being held for a new company called Ballet Theatre (now American Ballet Theatre).

Founded in 1940 by a young ballet enthusiast named Richard Pleasant and the former Mordkin ballerina Lucia Chase, it had ambitious goals. Like Ballet Caravan, it set out to be an American company but there the similarity stopped. Ballet Theatre hoped to be a showcase for the old masterpieces of dance as well as the best of contemporary offerings. Three wings of dance were established, each with a resident choreographer. Anton Dolin, the English danseur noble, was in charge of classic dance; Antony Tudor, the English dancer-choreographer, headed the British wing; and Eugene Loring, the American dancer-choreographer, directed the American wing. In addition, Michel Fokine was to stage his own ballets. And there were to be separate performing groups of Spanish dancers, Black dancers, and the promise of a wing of modern dance.

The new company absorbed most of the old Mordkin company and added new choreographers and dancers. Among the choreographers were such distinguished names as Adolph Bolm, Agnes de Mille, Mikhail Mordkin, and Bronislava Nijinska. The principal dancers included Nana Gollner, Karen Conrad, Patricia Bowman, Annabelle Lyon, Nina Stroganova; among the male dancers were Bolm, Dolin, Loring, Tudor, Dollar, Leon Danielian, and Hugh Laing.

For the opening night of Ballet Theatre in January, Fokine staged a revised version of his *Les Sylphides*. With the brilliant production and performances that evening, a major American ballet company came into existence.

Alicia, back in New York in the spring of 1940, decided to try out for the company's corps de ballet. Though she had already performed in New York in small solo roles, she thought she could best learn the fundamentals of the ballets, the music, and movement, in the corps.

She auditioned before three judges: Anton Dolin, Antony Tudor, and Eugene Loring. Of the many young hopefuls that day, four were selected: John Kriza, Muriel Bentley, Jerome Robbins—and Alicia Alonso.

Anton Dolin sums up best the value of the four new dancers to Ballet Theatre. In his *Autobiography* he wrote, "It turned out to be a lucky day, not only for the four dancers but for Ballet Theatre." They added, he said, to "its history and glory."

A few months later Fernando was accepted into the corps of the company.

In the backstage closeness of the dancers, Alicia found a new camaraderie. There were old friends Nora Kaye and Maria Karnilova as well as Jerome Robbins. And there were new friends. Among them none of the rivalries existed that would develop in the company in future years. The members of the company were supportive and affectionate and shared their concerns over small worries—"Did I do it right?" or "What went wrong?" Ballet Theatre became the most important thing in Alicia's life. She would say later that she lived only for ballet. This spirit flowed among the young dancers who had an undreamed-of opportunity to work with the top choreographers and star ballet dancers of the day. They dedicated themselves to Ballet Theatre and gave the company a rare unity in its first years.

With the start of rehearsals, Alicia found a new teacher, Alexandra Fedorova, who shared a studio near the temporary home of Ballet Theatre with her son, Leon Fokine.

In Fedorova, Alicia at last found the teacher of ballet classics who would help shape her style. There was immediate mutual affection between them. Fedorova saw in Alicia a young girl of promise, ready for hard work. "There was something inside her, in her heart," Fedorova said later, "that made me realize this was a determined girl."

Fedorova taught in the Cecchetti method she herself had learned at the Russian Imperial Dance School in Petrograd. Married to the brother of Michel Fokine, she was part of that charmed inner circle of great dancers which included Pavlova, Karsavina, Legat, and so many others. She had come to New York in 1937 from Latvia, where she had helped organize the National Ballet.

In Fedorova's classes and in classes with her son, Alicia's natural talent and technical skill were disciplined by daily, demanding exercises. It was not enough for Fedorova that Alicia's extensions and arabesques were spectacular. She had to learn the proper carriage, and the position of the body, and how to move; steps had to flow, one into the other.

"Dance with your whole body," Fedorova would say. "Use your feet and your arms—the arms are the most important because they are the ends of the body. Use them."

Leon Fokine taught Alicia character dancing, how to do the mazurkas and the czardas. When Alicia was short of money and could not pay for lessons, Fedorova would say, "Don't worry, you pay when you can."

Alicia's days were a round of classes, rehearsals, and performances. She took as many classes as she could crowd into a busy day. Her friends laughed at her as she rushed from one class to another. But she lived for those classes and for the world of ballet. When she was resting, she read books on dance.

She danced with Ballet Theatre for the first time in Philadelphia's Robin Hood Dell in June 1940. She was in the ensemble of Fokine's *Les Sylphides* and in Mordkin's *Voices of Spring.* And in a heavy schedule of ballets at New York's Lewisohn Stadium during the summer, she was in corps roles, dancing with Ballet Theatre for the first time in New York in *Voices of Spring.*

By mid-July she was given small ensemble roles. Tudor made her one of the friends and relations in his *Jardin aux Lilas.* He selected her as one of four cygnets for the pas de quatre in *Swan Lake.*

In early August she stepped into her first solo role with Ballet Theatre. Annabelle Lyon became ill and could not perform in *Peter and the Wolf* so Alicia danced the highly regarded role of the bird. John Martin of the *New York Times* gave Alicia her first press notice as solo dancer.

"As the bird," he wrote, she "showed herself to be a promising young artist with an easy technique, a fine sense of line and a great deal of youthful charm."

The glory of Ballet Theatre in its first years was its corps de ballet. Critic Olga Maynard called a few of its dancers "the equal—and sometimes the superior—of some Diaghilev soloists." In that category she placed Kaye, Karnilova, Bentley, Robbins, and "a Cuban dancer named Alicia Alonso."

In the fall of 1940 Alicia and Ballet Theatre departed for Chicago for a six-week season with the Chicago Opera Company. There she danced the regular repertory, including *Peter and the Wolf* and Loring's *Great American Goof.* In the Chicago premier of José Fernández's *Goyescas,* a ballet based on Goya's drawings, she and Nora Kaye danced two *majas,* attractive, provocative young women.

Back in New York for the 1941 spring season, Alicia felt completely integrated into the company. She continued her steady progress. The three leading choreographers selected her for significant roles. Tudor made her a resident coryphée (minor soloist) in his satiric ballet, *Gala Performance*. Dolin cast her in the distinguished role of Carlotta Grisi in *Pas de Quatre*. Loring chose her over the company's soloists and stars to work with him in the dual roles of the mother and Mexican sweetheart in *Billy the Kid*, which she had danced for Ballet Caravan. He himself would dance the role of Billy.

Ballet Theatre needed additional rehearsal space. Loring found a former mansion on West Fifty-third Street off Fifth Avenue. There in a vast ballroom with crystal chandeliers and a marble staircase, Loring and Alicia worked on *Billy the Kid*.

The ballet, based on American folklore, tells the story of the opening of the frontier and the westward migration. In particular, it is about a legendary young killer and his own violent end in the vast wilderness. Aaron Copland wrote the vigorous, haunting score, based on Western and cowboy melodies.

Alicia was tireless in rehearsals, sharing Loring's interest in searching out details, digging into character and making it more than "steps to music." Loring explained to Alicia that he saw the Mexican sweetheart "as a woman of sensuous quality and warmth that would make Billy seek her out in the wide open territory in which he eventually was killed." Loring found that kind of sensuous warmth in Alicia. "She radiated a sense of sun," he said; "a kind of full-blooded honesty," that she projected into her dancing.

Billy the Kid was performed on opening night of Ballet Theatre's 1941 spring season. The critics applauded Alicia. Irving Kolodin wrote that she "did an exceptionally good job of the Mexican sweetheart." Rosalyn Krokover said Alicia "seemed to be able to encompass the remoteness of a dream and the vitality of a warm, tender woman . . . [she] offered an extra dimension that made her sweetheart unique."

From then on, the critics commented regularly on Alicia's progress. Onstage her appearance was arresting. The soft roundness of her body and arms projected a languorous quality, but at the same time her dancing was sharp, clean, distinctive. She brightened her corner of the stage with the authority of her dancing, making each step, no matter how small, significant.

In her broadened repertory, John Martin noted that her performance in the *Swan Lake* pas de trois "was marked by fine technical proficiency and elegance of style. Here is a young artist of genuine parts who is eminently worth watching." And Walter Terry, later in February, mentioned that "Nora Kaye and Alicia Alonso dance as soloists with equal ease and I am willing to bet both of them will attain ballerina positions."

It was as Carlotta Grisi in Anton Dolin's version of *Pas de Quatre* that Alicia's star quality projected itself across the footlights.

The ballet tells the true story of four outstanding ballerinas of the romantic age who were brought together one hundred years ago by choreographers Coralli and Perrot in a dance called *Pas de Quatre*. Because of their intense rivalry, it was an extraordinary achievement to persuade Marie Taglioni, Lucile Grahn, Carlotta Grisi, and Fanny Cerrito to dance together. The choreographers provided each dancer with a solo to display her outstanding gifts as well as ensemble dancing that showed off all four together to great advantage.

Carlotta Grisi, married to choreographer Perrot, had already triumphed as Giselle when the ballet was premiered in Paris in 1841. And one hundred years later, Alicia Alonso, who would become a great Giselle herself, would perform as Grisi in *Pas de Quatre*. Alicia had a natural feeling for the romantic era and for Grisi, who was known for her love of dancing and her spectacular technique.

Alicia's performance that evening was enchanting. In rapid footwork, she moved diagonally across the stage with small steps en pointes. And when she turned to beats, they were clean, fine, like an etching or like the clear trill notes on a piano.

Pas de Quatre with Nana Gollner, Nina Stroganova, and Katherine Sergava joining Alicia in the lead roles, received seventeen curtain calls. Later, summing up the spring season, the reviewer of *Musical Courier* said, "Some individual performances are not easily forgotten. Alicia Alonso in *Pas de Quatre* was one of them."

Alicia's swift progress sometimes unnerved her. She felt, she later said, as if "she were drinking champagne and getting bubbles in her head." Then she would remember Loring's advice when he gave her an autographed photograph she had requested. Be careful of speedy success, he advised her. "You could get lost in it." It always made her pause and take stock. She would look around at her colleagues and remind herself not only to remember them but to value them.

Alicia continued to perform to accolades. John Martin had already predicted she would take her place with Markova and Pavlova. And in March, he mused in the *Times* about his favorite dancers:

"There is Alicia Alonso, on whom this department is laying its money heavily. Unless all signs fail, here is truly a classic dancer, in the sense that Alicia Markova is a classic dancer. Her exquisite performance of Carlotta Grisi in Anton Dolin's *Pas de Quatre* is no less than a forewarning that before long she is going to step with full grace into Grisi's most famous role of Giselle."

But before the season was over, Alicia had to attend to a difficulty that worried her. She was bumping into things during rehearsals and, worse, during performances. She thought vaguely it might be her eyesight. She played a game with Fernando to see who bumped into more things. It soon became clear there was something wrong with the focus of her eyes.

She was put under the care of a physician. He was in the audience one night when she became seriously ill during a performance. She saw black spots before her eyes and became dizzy. Fetched backstage, the doctor asked to see her in his office the next day. There he broke the news. Alicia was suffering from detached retina of the right eye and must enter the hospital immediately for an operation.

She performed in a full program the last evening of Ballet Theatre's spring season. She did the pas de trois in *Swan Lake* with her good friends Leon Danielian and Nina Stroganova. She was the Mexican sweetheart and the mother in Loring's *Billy the Kid* to Loring's Billy, and she was the resident coryphée in *Gala Performance*.

The next day she entered the hospital.

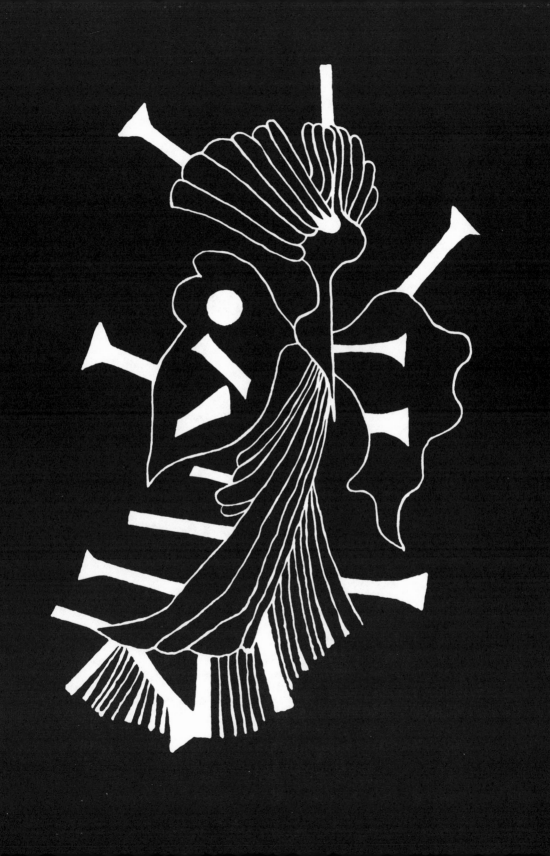

Alicia, Margit de Kova, Lew Christensen, and Fernando Alonso in
Charade

Alicia and Fernando rehearsing in their first New York apartment
(opposite page)   53

Alicia Alonso, Alicia Markova, Nora Kaye, and Janet Reed in *Pas de Quatre*

Alicia and Fernando in *Waltz Academy* (opposite page)

Carmelita Maracci with Angela Velez, Alicia Alonso, and Charlyne Baker
rehearsing *Circo de España*

Nora Kaye, Alicia Alonso, and Norma Vance in *Gala Performance*
(opposite page)

Alicia with John Kriza in *Billy the Kid*

Alicia and Hugh Laing in *Undertow* (top)

Alicia in *Les Sylphides* (opposite page)

Alicia in *Caprichos*

Nora Kaye, Jerome Robbins, Anton Dolin, Dimitri Romanoff, Annabelle
Lyon, Lucia Chase, Leon Danielian, Alicia Alonso, and other members of
Ballet Theatre in *Capricioso* (opposite page)

61

Alicia with John Kriza and Edward Caton in *La Fille Mal Gardée*

Alicia in *Fall River Legend* **(opposite page)**

Alicia in *Don Quixote*

Alicia with André Eglevsky in the Bluebird pas de deux from *Princess Aurora* (opposite page)

Eric Braun, John Kriza, Ruth Ann Koesun, and Alicia on the Piazza San Marco, Venice, Italy

Portrait

6

Dancing Is Over

$\mathcal{A}$licia lay in bed in Columbia Presbyterian Hospital recovering from the operation on her right eye for detached retina. An outstanding Spanish ophthalmologist practicing in New York City had performed the delicate surgery. Only his optimistic prognosis that she would be able to resume dancing eased Alicia's terrible fears. But he ordered her to lie quietly and not to move a muscle. It was thought at the time that immobilization of the body would enable the retina to settle back.

Overnight the vigorous dancer had been stilled. It was difficult not to move her legs. Ballet Theatre friends visiting her days later found her in bed, stretching her feet and legs under the covers in familiar ballet exercises. She assured them she would soon be back in the company.

The nurses, however, knew the fright that engulfed the young patient. Head nurse Ethel Pritchard, drawn to the lovely girl, took special care of her. Under her soothing ministrations and with the cheerful support of the hospital staff, Alicia had a comfortable recovery.

But Alicia and Fernando had every reason to worry. The retina is the sensory membrane over the eye which receives the first image. Even though the surgery was successful, the retinal tear left Alicia with diminished vision. She permanently lost the peripheral or side vision in her right eye. It was this loss which caused her to bump into things, for she could no longer see people or objects to the right or to the left without turning her head fully in that direction. The dark spots before her eyes were caused by a hemorrhage which accompanied the retinal tear.

The Ballet Theatre season was over, but there were classes. Alicia's joy in returning to them was short-lived, for the same symptoms soon reappeared.

Again the retina in her right eye had detached. Again she underwent surgery in Columbia Presbyterian Hospital. But this time her doctor advised her to return to Cuba for a lengthy rest. She was told she must stay quiet and avoid all exercises in order that her eye might fully heal.

Alicia returned at once to Cuba with Fernando and, at her family's insistence, visited their physician. He took her to a well-trained Cuban ophthalmologist. The medical report completely stunned her: she again had a detached retina of the right eye—and this time of the left eye as well. She was ordered into the hospital in Havana immediately for surgery on both eyes. Moreover, the ophthalmologist believed that any infection in the body might affect the eye. Since Alicia's tonsils were infected, he advised that they be removed.

Alicia was in no condition to make decisions. She put herself in the hands of her family, whose deepest concern was for her health. No one discussed her career as a dancer.

After the surgery, she was taken to the home of her mother-in-law, Laura Rayneri de Alonso, for her convalescence. There, in a large room she knew well but could not see, she lived for months in the dark world of the sightless.

"You must not cry, you must not laugh, you must not move," she was ordered. She heard the admonition over and over as she lay ill, eyes heavily bandaged. For the first few months weights were placed around her head at night to make sure she did not move it during her sleep.

The doctors concluded that Alicia never again would be able to dance. At most, they agreed, she could lead a simple life and perform a few chores. No one could bear to tell her that the most important part of her life was over. But the remarks of her attentive family, especially of her mother who would sit and hold her hand, gradually penetrated the haze of her mind. She would never be able to dance again.

Never? She was nineteen years old. What does Never mean? Alicia would not believe it. In the weeks and months of lying blinded, motionless, she realized that she had always lived to dance and that she would never stop. Even while lying still in bed she was dancing. With her eyes closed, she danced in her mind. She kept working for something inside her that she could not let die.

Alicia rehearsed daily in her head and with her fingertips. She worked on one ballet in particular—*Giselle*. It was the dance of her convalescence and that was probably why she later would love it so much. Each day she listened to the music of Adolphe Adam until it reached deep inside. Her fingers became nimble, expert, as she shaped them into an arabesque, folded them into a plié, or stretched them into a jeté.

Using the bedsheet as a stage, she performed for Fernando each evening so that he could correct her errors and tell her which way to turn. She learned other dances and developed her prodigious memory. In her fantasies she was not blind, helpless Alicia lying bandaged in bed but a ballerina soaring into space in a happy village dance. Or more aptly, she was like the wili, a spirit, in the ballet *Giselle* fighting for the life of her true love.

In June the news came from New York that critic John Martin had placed her on his Honor Roll. It cheered her, although the irony of it did not go unnoticed. His selections were based not only on past performance but on the dancer's *future* promise.

Alicia Alonso was his choice, he wrote, "especially for her role of Carlotta Grisi in *Pas de Quatre* and in general for the rare elegance and beauty of her classic style and in her performance of even the most modest bits in other ballets."

The bad days continued when it was torture to lie in bed. In spite of doctors' orders, she let three-year-old Laura steal into the room. They played together, Alicia pretending she could see her daughter. But as the months wore on, she felt her body grow fat and flabby. She could feel her dancer's muscles wasting away.

The day finally came when the bandages were removed. She opened her eyes. The lids seemed so heavy that her first thought was, "My God, how can people keep their eyes open all the time?" Then she saw the sky and the bright colors around her. "It is so beautiful," she said.

Only Alicia and the family knew the full extent of the damage to her vision.

In her right eye, operated on three times, she had lost vision to the side, down and up, leaving her with tunnel vision only. And that was further damaged by permanent scars. She saw only pieces of an image as if she were looking out through a badly scratched windowpane.

In her left eye she lost some vision to one side.

For a dancer, Alicia knew that she had suffered a great tragedy. As she often said, "A ballerina learns with her eyes, watching others dance." Alicia had to learn to walk again. She had to learn to see again. And she had to overcome fear.

When she got out of bed, she could not stand by herself. She had lost all sensation in her legs. Fernando held on to one arm; her sister held the other. Someone stood in back of her and moved her legs in the rhythm of walking until she regained the reflex action.

When she finally began to get around, she could only walk very slowly. At her twentieth birthday celebration in December, she tried to be cheerful. That month the Martha Graham Dance Company arrived in Havana to perform at Pro Arte. Three dancers were housed at the lovely home of Alicia's sister, by then married. Others were guests at the home of Laura Rayneri de Alonso, whom they affectionately called "La Grande Dame" of Havana. One of them remembered Alicia attending rehearsals, always quiet and sad-looking. They sympathized with the talented young Alicia whose bright future, they thought, had been tragically brought to an end.

But as Alicia regained her strength, she set other plans into motion. She decided that she had listened to the doctors long enough. In early 1942, she returned to Pro Arte. Again changes had taken place. Laura Rayneri was still the creative administrator but the head of the ballet school was now Alberto Alonso.

Alicia found a rehearsal room at Pro Arte where she could work alone. For a full year she had not been near a barre. She started with simple basic exercises. If in her impatience she worked too hard, her legs cramped. Then she knew she had to pace herself, to do a bit each day or she would injure her muscles.

She held on to the barre to do her first jump. It was a small jump but pain shot through her legs as if she had no feet and was jumping on her ankles. She worked at moving an arm and a leg at the same time; on moving her head separately from her body. She formed a bad habit with her head, straining and stretching it forward, which would take years to overcome.

But she had to do more than retrain her body. She had to accommodate to a new sense of space. When she tried to bring together a finger of each hand, they would not meet. Only by doing it over and over, slowly, could she work through the margin of change.

These were small things. There were pirouettes, fouettés, soaring leaps. Her patience and determination did justice to Beethoven, her favorite composer, who wrote some of his greatest music after becoming totally deaf.

Alicia gradually expanded her activities. In La Silva, a short-lived but significant organization, Alicia joined writers, composers, dancers, and other creative artists who met together to talk and to pool their abilities. Through their encouragement, Alicia did her first choreographic work—the ballet *La Condesita*, with music by Joaquín Nin, based on an anonymous Spanish romance and produced at Pro Arte.

The ballet school at Pro Arte, under Alberto Alonso, was also having a burst of creative activity. There was considerable talent among its 150 students and its teaching staff. Foremost was Alicia's sister, Cuca. There was also her talented friend, Leonor Albarrán. Alberto Alonso, Fernando Alonso, and Alberto's wife, Alexandra Denisova (a Canadian who had changed her name from Patricia Denise in keeping with the Russian craze of the day) both taught and danced. When a small opera company arrived on tour from New York, Alicia staged the dances for *Aida*.

She began to teach a dancing class at the exclusive School of Language and Art. And teaching, she knew, was only a step away from dancing.

In mid-1942 Alicia became a guest artist at Pro Arte. She had not discussed it with her physician but simply began to dance. She did the pas de deux in *Aurora's Wedding*, and later on she danced in *Les Sylphides*. She also performed in many of Alberto's original choreographic works. There was, among others, *La Hija del General*, to music by Johann Strauss, as well as his *Concerto* to music by Vivaldi-Bach.

Alicia was at home one day when a hurricane swept over Havana. She ran out to the patio to fetch her Great Dane and its newly born puppies. A howling wind threw her down over the puppies and shattered the glass door. Splinters of glass cut gashes in Alicia's head. Blood covered her eyes. "Oh God, my eyes!" she screamed. Fernando rushed out and found Alicia lying on the ground.

The doctor reassured her that only her head had been cut. Her eyes had not been injured.

"Can I dance?" she asked, demanding his permission. "Since the blow did no damage to my eyes, can I *really* return to ballet?"

The doctor pondered her question. His answer was slow in coming. "It's up to you," he finally said.

It was enough for Alicia. She wired Lucia Chase, director of Ballet Theatre in New York, "I am ready to return."

7

A New Giselle

$\mathcal{A}$licia saw how much the city had changed when she returned to New York in the fall of 1943. The bleakness of the Depression years had given way to the vigor and bustle of a country fighting a war. People rushed along the streets with a velocity that reminded her of a tropical storm in Cuba.

She made her way at once to Ballet Theatre headquarters in the West Fifty-third Street townhouse. Director Lucia Chase warmly greeted her. She was glad to have one of her favorite ballet dancers back in the company.

Alicia and Fernando quickly settled into an apartment, again on the West Side. She could take a bus or a subway the short distance to class and to rehearsals at the Metropolitan Opera House on Seventh Avenue and Thirty-ninth Street, where the company regularly performed.

It took only a few days for Alicia to become immersed in the fall ballet season. Between classes and rehearsals she tried to catch up on changes in the company. It was hardly the same one she had left two and a half years before.

What struck her was the unusual glamour and excitement, especially over the new prima ballerinas Alicia Markova and Irina Baronova. Along with Anton Dolin, often their partner, they ranked as stars.

The two primas had been added by a new management. In July 1941 Ballet Theatre signed a contract with Sol Hurok Enterprises. Hurok had a well-deserved reputation as an astute businessman and manager who could make companies flourish at the box office. He loudly proclaimed Ballet Theatre to be "the most promising company in the Western world." Then he proceeded to restructure it in the image of Ballet Russe de Monte Carlo, which he also managed.

At once, Ballet Theatre's simple, open face changed. Instead of listing the dancers as a single group headed unobtrusively by the principals, Hurok established the old system of star billing. He also brought in the regisseur, the peculiarly European type of manager who supervises the complex details of rehearsals and performances. Above all, he advertised Ballet Theatre as "the greatest in Russian ballet," or "Ballet Theatre with its repertoire of Russian ballet for American audiences." The key word was "Russian." American genre ballet remained but as a token commitment. Agnes de Mille was still attached to the company. And Jerome Robbins began work on what has become an American classic, *Fancy Free*.

Under Hurok, Ballet Theatre became big business. Attendance shattered previous records. In the summer of 1943, the Hollywood Bowl with its 22,000 seats was sold out for eight performances.

Alicia found new tensions backstage, and intrigue that had not been there before. Though she appreciated its vitality, she missed the company's former simplicity.

She also missed old friends. The bright, creative Eugene Loring had departed over program disagreements. For a couple of years he had his own New York company, Dance Players. Then he settled on the West Coast and became an influential figure there in ballet and theater.

A friend from early corps days, Donald Saddler, had gone off to the war, along with many others. And though she had not personally known Michel Fokine well, his death in New York in 1942 had been a severe blow.

She had joyful reunions with the friends who remained—Nora Kaye, Maria Karnilova, Robbins, Laing, and Kriza. André Eglevsky and Michael Kidd were now in the company. There were new faces: Rosella Hightower, Barbara Fallis, Janet Reed, Sono Osato, and Leonide Massine.

Antony Tudor was still there, creating gripping, tension-filled ballets that drew unexpected qualities from dancers. Nora Kaye, with a rare, dramatic style, became an overnight sensation in Tudor's *Pillar of Fire*. And Lucia Chase was there as both dancer and administrator, trying to steer the company on a middle course between Hurok's drive to Europeanize it and its original intent of developing an American posture.

But the star of the company was Alicia Markova. The English-born prima had been trained in London by Seraphine Astafieva, another of the Russian emigré teachers who shaped a generation of Western dancers. Diaghilev accepted Markova into his company at age fourteen. Cecchetti, then maestro for Diaghilev, added to her technical skills. And the elegance of the fabled company shaped her style. At a young age she became a star. With Anton Dolin, whose background was similar, an exciting dance partnership was born. Unable to return to their own war-torn England, they stayed on in the United States, adding their special romantic style to Ballet Theatre.

Alicia had first seen Markova in 1940. She was dancing the lead in *Giselle* at the Metropolitan Opera House and for the first time the novice from Cuba grasped the full romanticism of that classic ballet. Now in 1943, Alicia herself was rehearsing with Markova for *Pas de Quatre*, with Hightower and Reed in the other roles. And as they rehearsed, Alicia Alonso again marveled at Markova's lightness and the economy of her movements, the way she used her legs, arms, and head at the same time without a wasteful motion.

The company had changed, the city had changed, and so had she. The twenty-one-year-old ballet dancer who rejoined the company in 1943 was no longer a frightened young girl clinging to her husband. Gone was the youthful romanticism with which she first came to New York. She had matured. She was still fun-loving, her large smile lighting up her face, the low husky voice probing for English words. She moved with poise. She had elegance and pride, a new national pride. During her long convalescence in Havana, she had met creative artists, poets, painters, composers. Their efforts to shape a Cuban culture that would blend together the country's rich traditions deepened her respect for them as well as for her country.

She had had months and years in which to think while she struggled against blindness. She wanted now only to work and dance. For the fall season at the Metropolitan Opera House, she rehearsed new roles and performed with new dancers. On opening night she did a gypsy dance with Jerome Robbins in Massine's *Capriccio Espagnol*. She was also one of six fairies in the *Princess Aurora* divertissement, with Dolin and Markova in the leads.

Reviewers noted Alicia's return. John Martin commented in the *Times* that "the distinguishing feature of [*Capriccio Espagnol*] was the return to the company of Alicia Alonso after an absence of three years. It is good to have her back for she is a delightful dancer."

A young dancer at the beginning of her own brilliant career, Maria Tallchief, finding her way around New York City, also noticed Alicia. Tallchief wrote home to her family on the West Coast that there were wonderful Americans in Ballet Theatre—Janet Reed, Nora Kaye, Michael Kidd, and a "Cuban dancer Alicia Alonso."

To Alicia, watching and learning were lifetime habits. She stood in the wings and observed Markova and Dolin work on *Giselle.* The Dolin version had turned that classic into a box-office success. Alicia knew the music thoroughly, and she knew every role. She had performed it in her head a thousand times, acting out its dramatic moments and floating along on its lightness as if she were dancing on a cloud. In her fantasies she was a great Giselle, although in reality, she had danced only fragments of it.

In late October, Alicia Markova became ill and had to cancel her scheduled performance of *Giselle.*

Anton Dolin approached the three ranking ballet dancers, Rosella Hightower, Nora Kaye, and Alicia Alonso and asked each one if she could do *Giselle.* Both Hightower and Kaye said they could not do it. But Alicia quickly replied, "Yes, I can," forgetting that she had never actually performed it.

With only five days until the performance, Alicia and Dolin, who was to dance the role of the prince, rehearsed in a large room on an upper floor of the Metropolitan Opera House. Dolin, with infinite patience, taught her the steps, movements, and acting of a role often considered the most demanding in ballet. The magic of *Giselle* is produced by the dancers who must have the dramatic talent and sensitivity to make the story credible and give it universal meaning.

Based on a German legend, the ballet tells the story of Giselle, a country maiden in a Rhineland village who is wooed by the young Prince Albrecht, disguised as a peasant. When his identity is revealed, Giselle dies of shock and grief. She is turned into a wili, the fate of young betrothed girls who die of unrequited love. The wilis haunt the forests at night forcing men who wander through the woodlands into an endless dance until they die from exhaustion. Albrecht, visiting Giselle's grave, is spared this fate by Giselle's love and faith.

The Metropolitan Opera House was filled the evening of November 2. Many in the audience had read of Markova's illness and knew she would be replaced. Nevertheless, it was with deep misgivings that Dolin appeared in front of the curtain to announce the change in cast. To his relief, the audience reacted calmly.

The great golden damask curtains parted that evening on a village scene, and the familiar story unfolded: Prince Albrecht is seen assuming his peasant guise. He raps on the door of a cottage and hides. Giselle, gay, laughing, runs out of the cottage hoping to find the handsome peasant who had wooed her. In a brief, happy dance she establishes her tender feelings, her fragility, as she shows hope, disappointment, and then her immense joy when Albrecht laughingly joins her.

And Alicia Alonso, in her first leading role in a ballet classic, and one strongly identified with Markova, showed a cheering audience that she had the technique, style, and dramatic ability of a classical dancer. Dolin was proud of her "remarkable first performance." And Martin wrote that it was "one of the most distinguished performances of the season. . . . Miss Alonso acquitted herself with brilliance."

For Alicia, it fulfilled a dream—just to dance *Giselle*. It was not the beginning fame that thrilled her. She was "too knocked out," she would say later, to feel happy or surprised. "I danced it because I liked it," she said.

But despite acclaim for her *Giselle*, she did not leap forward into other star roles. One did not rise from the ranks that quickly. She found herself in her usual repertory of small solo roles and the classics were still performed by the prima Markova.

Alicia resumed classes with Fedorova. She had studied with many fine teachers and would always pay tribute to the skill of Shollar, Vladimiroff, Vilzak, Volkova, and others, but it was with Fedorova that she worked hardest. She had long ago learned that talent was not enough. There was no mystery to becoming a dancer. It required hard work, day after day, including holidays, in an endless grind of exercises. She worked alone and she worked in class, disciplined and determined to improve each step, to do four turns instead of three. As a result of her prodigious effort, she began to master her technique and could use it to express herself the way an artist uses paint on a canvas. The more she learned, the more she could say, combining her movements into eloquent statements. With her feet blistered, ligaments torn, limp with exhaustion, she continued to work.

Sometimes, watching the ballerinas, she despaired of ever reaching the pinnacle. "I'll never be that good," she would say. At other times, unhappy over her performance, she would run into the wings, complaining, "I was terrible."

When the stardust had settled after her single performance as Giselle, she could see how much she had imitated Markova. That was the way she had learned it. In the months that followed, she thought about that performance and she knew she would perform it differently if she ever had the chance.

The studio where she spent her time with Fedorova and Leon Fokine was more than a place to learn technique and style. Fedorova, a remarkable woman, had one heroine—Pavlova. Fedorova recalled Pavlova's willingness to work hard. She had persuaded Cecchetti to give up his private school and to work exclusively with her to help her overcome some technical difficulties. He imposed on Pavlova a rigid schedule of exercises that continued for three years. Each day of each week was devoted to specific exercises to overcome a specific problem in technique.

No one Alicia knew had the luxury of such specialized training. Neither she nor any American-trained dancer had the advantage of the structured dance education that existed in Russia. Then, as today, talented children, starting at age ten, were put into a dance school designed to teach ballet as if it were a natural part of growth. It produced some of the greatest ballet dancers in the world.

Alicia, from her first days in dance school, had to exert her own drive and determination. She had to impose her own self-discipline. Above all, she had to search for teachers who could help her fashion her own style of dancing. In a broad sense, untouched by any godmother's wand, she *created* her own style of dancing. And it was always undergoing change. One evening she danced a role one way.

The next evening it would be different. She thought, probed, and experimented.

Performance days had their established routine. She took class, rehearsed both alone and with the company and made the last two hours before a performance her own. During that time she became a Carlotta Grisi, a cygnet, and in later years, a Giselle or Princess Aurora. To each role she brought the unique intensity that characterized her even as a child.

A reporter in Boston came up against this intense concentration. Sent to do a story on the young dancer performing with Ballet Theatre at the Boston Opera House, she found Alicia rehearsing for her role as the bird in *Peter and the Wolf*. Alicia talked with the reporter for a few minutes and then explained she had to "warm up" for her role. The reporter wrote in amazement that "warming up" for a role she already knew was more important to the little-known dancer than publicity in a newspaper. But before she left, Alicia said to the reporter in her halting English, "To see, to dance, it is so beautiful. . . . It took patience, great patience [to get well]. But now I am so very grateful. . . . I know God does not intend I take for granted these gifts, to see, to dance. . . . I love them so very much."

As Alicia learned more, she began to put more of herself into her roles, making them richer, fuller. They radiated with warmth and beauty. Perhaps because of her damaged eyesight, she paid great attention to detail. She sharpened the edge of her dancing until it sparkled with shafts of brilliance like the sun glinting on the sea.

None of this was lost on either audiences or reviewers. On many occasions writers thanked her for making an otherwise dull evening worthwhile.

In October 1944 dance critic Edwin Denby wrote: "The event of the evening was Alicia Alonso's dancing . . . she triumphed by her purity of style in three different ballets." He described her mazurka in *Les Sylphides* as "perfection in the quick accuracy of leaps, in the lovely bearing of chest, shoulder and head, and in the rapid and exact tripping toe steps. . . ."

And John Martin wrote at the end of 1944 that Alicia was dancing better than she had ever danced before. "She has line and lightness, brilliance and authority and a true sense of the classic style. . . . There is a quality of excitement about her dancing that marks only the great classicists.''

Alicia was disappointed she was not called on to do *Giselle* again in New York. There were so many ways she would do it differently. But she was grateful just to be dancing. Fears about her eyes often leaped out of dark shadows—she could hear the voice of the doctor, like an executioner, intoning fateful words, cutting her down in mid-career.

So Alicia had her own private chart for measuring the value of her days. But she was not unaware of ballet politics and the whisperings backstage as frustration mounted among talented dancers waiting to dance lead roles. She kept up with the talk.

Alicia's chance to step into classical roles had come, everyone said, when Markova and Dolin left Ballet Theatre at the end of 1944 to perform with the company only as special guests. But instead, Hurok brought in a new group of glittering European dancers. Heading them as prima ballerina was Tamara Toumanova. There were also Riabouchinska, Massine, and Lichine. They were strong, often brilliant dancers. But something went wrong. The company no longer hung together. Its center of unity was gone as if it turned with a broken spoke. Dance writers were outspoken in their criticism of Ballet Theatre. It lacked a "definable policy," said John Martin. More than that, talented dancers like Gollner, Alonso, Reed, Kaye, Hightower were being neglected. These dancers "if developed according to their ability would lead the company to undreamed-of standards of achievement," he said.

Despite the frustrations, Alicia's career moved ahead. In early 1945, Tudor selected her to create a dramatic role in his new ballet *Undertow*, to music by William Schuman. It tells the searing story of a young man's defeat by the estranging and corrupt forces that surround him from birth on. As Ate, Alicia dances the role of a wanton, aggressive girl who is raped by four vicious street toughs. Tudor drew from Alicia her sensuality and used it full-blown as it had never before been seen on the stage. Through her agile movements, phrasing, the way she stood, the way she looked with curled, matted hair, she became the shameless, terribly damaged Ate.

"Go to see Alicia Alonso in *Undertow*," critics advised the public in mixed reviews about the ballet itself. Her "magnificent bit" gave the sorely troubled Ballet Theatre box office a needed lift. There was pressure again on the company to use its American dancers. The public recognized them as prima ballerinas but Hurok, tied to his European stars, continued to place the American dancers in secondary roles.

Finally, Alicia's big moment was announced for the fall of 1945. She and André Eglevsky were to perform in *Giselle* in New York. On tour, she had danced the role with Hugh Laing except in large cities where Dolin and Markova had the leads.

Alicia's picture was splashed over the newspapers announcing the forthcoming performance. She had developed a considerable following that rated her the best classical dancer in New York, despite the great publicity given primas favored by Hurok. On the long-awaited evening, the Metropolitan Opera House quickly filled. The audience that night saw a different Giselle. Alicia had moved away from her first model, Markova. In the first act she was warm, vivid, direct. She had no guile, only the purity and passion of a young village girl in love. In the second act, she developed the elusiveness of the ghostly wili, and throughout there was the magnificent dancing of Alonso and Eglevsky together, convincing an enthusiastic audience once again that faith can conquer even death.

8

"A True Ballerina"

No longer was there any doubt where Alicia Alonso belonged in Ballet Theatre. Her technique, the style and temperament she brought to roles, made her its great classic dancer.

In New York and on tour Alicia performed in an expanded repertory which included Balanchine's *Waltz Academy*, and *Apollo*, and Tudor's *Romeo and Juliet*. She danced with Eglevsky in a new pas de deux created by Anatole Oboukhoff, and in *Spectre de la Rose*, *The Bluebird* pas de deux, and in John Taras's *Graziana*. On tour she danced with guest artists Dolin and Markova in *Les Sylphides* and with Markova in *Pas de Quatre*.

In the spring of 1946 a change at the top created a new atmosphere in the company. Hurok's tenure ended, and Lucia Chase and scenic designer-artist Oliver Smith became co-directors. Quickly they shed the Russian image Hurok had fostered and thrust Ballet Theatre forward once again as an American company. Except for Eglevsky, the leading dancers were all American-trained—Alonso, Kaye, Reed, Kriza, Kidd. And they stepped at once into leading roles.

As if to celebrate its new face and posture, the company traveled abroad for the first time. In the summer of 1946, it performed in London at the Royal Opera House, Covent Garden. Shorn of its European glamour and standing pristine in its native simplicity, Ballet Theatre presented a repertory of the classics, modern ballet and, most importantly, two American choreographed ballets—Jerome Robbins's *Fancy Free* and *Interplay*.

Ballet Theatre played to packed houses in London. The smash hit was *Fancy Free*. The English critics saw in it qualities they associated with Americans: "vitality," "gusto," and the rich humor of New Yorkers "both crude and subtle."

They praised Alonso's "classical line . . . and the vital ethereal quality" she displayed in the second act of *Giselle,* though they had little enthusiasm generally for the company's presentation of the classics.

Back in the United States there was growing national pride in American ballet. The dancers had become exciting copy for newspapers and magazines, much as their European counterparts had been for years.

Alicia's brilliant performances won her a good share of publicity. Two years earlier, in 1944, *Life* magazine had featured her in a picture story illustrating basic ballet steps and scenes from ballets. In Havana Alicia's father bought up all the copies of the issue and handed them out to friends as if they were souvenirs. During the first year after Alicia's departure from Havana, he knew nothing about her dancing. Then she sent him a book of clippings. Impressed with her talent and success, he thereafter attentively followed her progress. Though it was not the life he had wanted for his daughter, he became reconciled to a career that made her happy.

In 1944, too, the magazine *Norte* had a cover picture of Alicia. *Newsweek* did a cover story on her with the comment that, "In Miss Alonso, the Western Hemisphere has found its most expressive classic ballerina." She was featured in dance magazines, in *Vogue,* and in regional periodicals and newspapers.

Then awards began coming her way. *Mademoiselle* magazine selected her as one of the outstanding women of 1946. "She is the first American classic ballerina, Cuban born, American bred," it said, with "a personal radiance, a perfect technical ability and an awareness of style long lacking in the American ballet dancer. . . . In 1946 her Giselle proved she had mastered the strict vocabulary of the classic ballet and joined the immortal company of Markova and Pavlova."

In 1947, the government of Alicia's own Cuba bestowed on her its highest civilian award, the decoration of Carlos Manuel de Cespedes. With it went the title of *Dama.* To further celebrate the event, a postage stamp with her picture was issued.

During her development into a ballerina, Alicia had learned the value of an outstanding partner. She thought of partnering as communication between two people. "In many ways it was like having a conversation," she was to say. "Two people are talking to each other. One is more romantic, more lyrical; it calls that up in you. One is more vivid, more dramatic; it calls that up in you and you dance accordingly."

Alicia had been partnered by many fine dancers—Loring, Dolin, Eglevsky, Laing, Kriza. But now she would dance with one of the greatest—the danseur noble Igor Youskevitch.

When Youskevitch joined Ballet Theatre and became Alicia's partner, there was the magic of two people talking, or dancing, as one.

"They had such perfection as a team," said Maria Karnilova, "as if they were born to dance together." They enriched each other's gifts, illuminating ballets with new spirit and elegance, lighting up the stages of Europe and the Americas with their virtuoso dancing and their deeply shared romanticism. He was always the prince supreme to her Sleeping Beauty, Juliet, Giselle, the enchanted Swan.

Their first performance together did not augur such a happy future. Youskevitch was scheduled to dance with Nora Kaye on the opening night of the 1946 fall season. But Miss Kaye had a busy schedule. Lucia Chase asked Youskevitch if he would like to dance with Alicia. "Alicia would be fine," he answered.

Youskevitch had seen Alicia dance as Ate in *Undertow* before he joined the company and he considered her a fine actress and a promising ballerina. He persuaded her to dance with him on opening night—and his first performance with the company—in the Black Swan pas de deux. Alicia, still learning the role, was reluctant to do so.

She did not dance it well that night. When the curtain came down she cried, blaming Youskevitch for her poor performance. Youskevitch understood her hurt. He assured her it was only a question of "getting it." In time it became one of their most brilliant pas de deux.

Youskevitch, when he joined Ballet Theatre, was at the peak of his artistry. He had prodigious technical skill and the gallantry and grace of bygone days. Though he was only three years old when his wealthy family spirited him out of Russia after the 1917 revolution, the courtliness of upper-class society left its mark on him. In exile, too, in a suburb of Belgrade, Yugoslavia, which became a haven for Russian emigrés, his family maintained its standing. At school, where he took a class in social dancing, another Russian emigré, Nikolai Yavorsky, was his teacher—the same Yavorsky who later became Alicia's first teacher.

The young Youskevitch became a gymnast of note. And then, persuaded by a Yugoslavian ballerina to partner her, he began to study ballet. He was fashioned into a danseur by another Russian emigré, Olga Preobrajenska, at her studio in Paris. For many years Youskevitch danced with Ballet Russe de Monte Carlo, partnering the prima ballerinas Alicia Markova, Alexandra Danilova, and others. During the war he served in the U.S. Navy. And then he became the danseur noble with Ballet Theatre, partnering their ballerinas, combining his elegance in particular with the elegance of Alicia Alonso.

It pleased Lucia Chase to see them together onstage; they seemed suited to each other in looks and temperament. But their naturalness resulted from hard work. They both found it important to discuss a ballet in detail, to plan it beforehand so that they knew its movements thoroughly. After each performance they would again talk to analyze why a step or movement was different from what they planned. Youskevitch had a scientific approach, a habit from his academic training as an engineer. Once a step was decided on, he preferred that it remain exactly that way.

But Alicia was like a painter filling in a canvas with the pattern of a dance and the position of the dancers. She was eager to experiment, to apply new colors and accents to her canvas. In dance she might try a movement one way one night and then change it for the second night, perhaps to reflect her mood that day.

"You held a balance too long," Youskevitch might complain after a performance.

Alicia would burst out, "Oh, please, let me dance! Let me dance! I don't want to think."

You can talk with a partner only up to a certain point, Alicia began to realize. You can sit and talk but then there must be a certain elasticity on stage in which both dancers are free to take advantage of the moment. If the conductor is slow that evening, and there is time for three pirouettes instead of the planned two, or if the ballerina holds her balance longer that evening, she should feel free to do so. If the male dancer is jumping brilliantly, then the ballerina must wait a little and give him his chance. Each should encourage the other to seize unexpected opportunities to be brilliant, to do a bravura step. This, she would say, was what gave performances life and spontaneity; otherwise they would be automatic, settled, like a watch—affecting the audience with their dullness.

These small differences did not interfere with the joy each found in the partnership, in their sharing of the music, or the tempo of the dance. Youskevitch admired Alicia's enormous natural gifts, her turnout, the brilliant use of her small, beautiful feet, the technical range that enabled her to dance any role. Alicia appreciated in Youskevitch not only his skill but his elegance, the grace of every gesture, his good taste. "He had the natural manner of a danseur noble," she would say.

With Youskevitch, who knew the handicap of her damaged eyesight, Alicia felt completely secure. Together they gave dazzling performances. Their special gifts were put into a ballet created for them by George Balanchine. Called *Theme and Variations*, to music by Tchaikovsky, it recalled a more traditional period of ballet at the time of the Russian Imperial Court. Woodman Thompson's elegant costumes and sets captured the grandeur of the period. In this abstract dance with its interweaving patterns between the two soloists and the ensemble, Balanchine drew on the virtuosity of Alonso and Youskevitch. They filled the stage with swift turns, sustained adagios and soaring leaps that ended in a complex and elaborate finale.

Balanchine was a challenging choreographer. In rehearsals he demanded that Alicia increase the momentum of her dancing. She did not know she could move that swiftly. Alicia saw that Balanchine spoke through technique, but it was technique tied to music. She learned from Balanchine the importance of music—to distinguish between instruments, and to recognize what instrument was providing the melody. A melody played on a violin inspired a different strength of movement from one played on a harp. Tudor's approach was different, she said. Working on his ballets, she had to understand the story and the personality of a character and then unfold it through the way she stood, moved, and danced. "Whatever you feel, say it with your body," Tudor would tell her.

With *Theme and Variations* Alicia Alonso became America's great classical ballerina. John Martin, who had seen her star quality when she took her first steps in the corps de ballet, acknowledged that the "promising artist has incontrovertibly given place to a true ballerina."

It was not only Alicia's technique that was formidable but also her dramatic range. Choreographers called on her ability to fill varied roles in the spring season of 1948 when they were preparing new ballets for their premieres.

De Mille was working on *Fall River Legend* and Tudor on *Shadow of the Wind*. Both ballets, listed as the great events of the season, were eagerly awaited. The two choreographers required rehearsal time with dancers and musicians that often conflicted. The air was electric with anxieties and bickering.

De Mille was depending on the special dramatic talent of Nora Kaye to create the lead role in *Fall River Legend*. A week before opening night, Miss Kaye became seriously ill. Lucia Chase asked Alicia Alonso to fill the role. There was one week to prepare for it and Alicia already had a heavy schedule of numbers, rehearsing in Tudor's *Shadow of the Wind* as well as his *Romeo and Juliet*. Alicia reluctantly agreed to do it with the understanding she would dance the role two or three times after opening night so that she could fully work out her interpretation.

The ballet is based on the story of Lizzie Borden, a New England woman reared in the narrow, religious atmosphere of a small town. When she was a child, her gentle mother died and her father remarried. Cruelly mistreated by her stepmother and an alienated father, Lizzie goes increasingly mad. One day, in rage and despair, Lizzie picks up an ax and murders her father and stepmother.

Alicia read everything she could find about Lizzie Borden and about the small town where the sensational murder had taken place. To grasp the substance of the woman—to get inside her—she pored over photographs and even ate what Lizzie Borden ate—mutton. Not only was the cruel murder difficult for Alicia to grasp but the style of dance was equally difficult. It used ballet technique, but the accent was down. Alicia had to learn to pull the weight of her body down, to press down into the ground, to feel the weight in her stomach. In classical ballet, Alicia danced with the accent technically up, in the air, to achieve lightness.

The heavy, dramatic story, the new technique, and the petty personal backstage intrigue during the ballet's preparation made Alicia tense and irritated. "What happened to that light? It didn't come on stage. What happened?" she would snap, upset if the smallest detail went wrong.

When the curtain opened on *Fall River Legend,* the stunning backdrop and sets by Oliver Smith evoked a narrow coldness of life. Morton Gould provided the musical score. And Alicia Alonso created the ballet's dramatic needs with her interpretation. She showed a gentle Lizzie with the mother she loved and then a fearful, despairing woman, assailed by hysteria and rage, driven to commit the crime.

There was a tremendous ovation, when the curtain fell, for the dancer, the choreographer, composer, and designer. But de Mille was disappointed, though she would later call Alicia's dancing "marvelous." Not until Nora Kaye performed in *Fall River Legend,* did de Mille feel the ballet's emotional force had been fulfilled.

By the 1948 season Alicia Alonso 's dancing clearly had progressed to a new level of brilliance. With her new sense of security, the stiffness of her neck and shoulders that had become a habit after her eye operations, melted away. Those critics who thought she sometimes interrupted the flow of movement by "jabbing at a stress," acknowledged the quietness and elegance of her dancing. She dominated the stage with buoyancy and power. Her technique was formidable, whether in batterie, pirouettes, attitudes, balances. She filled an extraordinary range of roles. As Odile, in the Black Swan pas de deux, which she mastered as Youskevitch had prophesied, she slashed the air with sabre-sharp extensions and whipped across the stage in pirouettes that glinted in precision. She was as delicate as a whispering leaf in *Giselle.* She was a wanton Ate, a demented Lizzie Borden, a lyrical Terpsichore in *Apollo.*

Ballet dancers, watching Alicia from the wings, saw in her their ideal of a romantic ballerina. Often her Giselle would bring tears to their eyes.

With her dark hair framing the pallor of her face and her large dark eyes, Alicia appeared soft and gentle. But within her was the strength of steel. She was simple and direct but she had great emotional force. She had a sense of comedy and of tragedy. All of it she fed into her dancing.

With Nora Kaye and Igor Youskevitch, Alicia Alonso became the mainstay of Ballet Theatre. She had helped it win an international reputation as a great American company in its first decade.

But despite its successes, the company was burdened with financial problems and, at the end of the spring 1948 performances, Lucia Chase announced there would be no 1949 season. The dancers were dismissed until further notice.

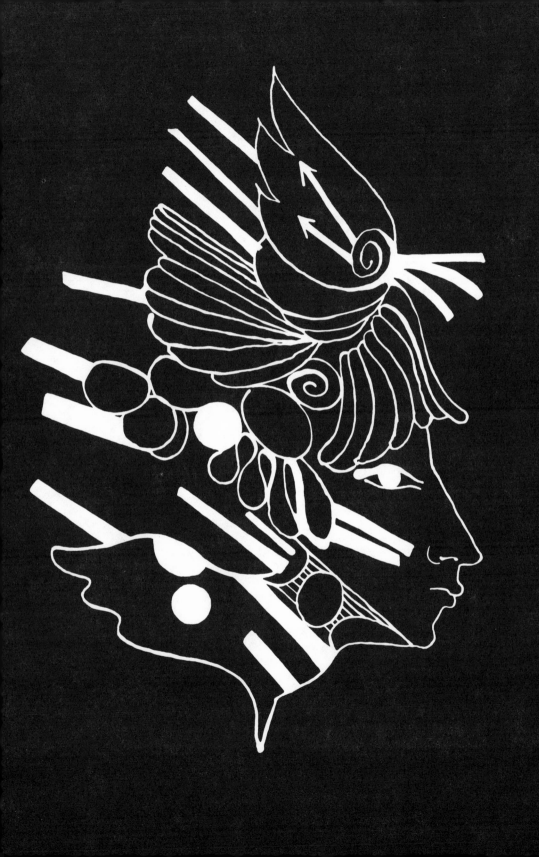

Alicia with Anton Dolin in her first *Giselle*, 1943

Giselle, Act I (opposite page)

With Azari Plisetski as Albrecht in *Giselle*, Act I

Giselle, Act I (opposite page)

Giselle, Act II

With Erik Bruhn in a pas de deux from *Giselle,* Act II, at Jacob's Pillow

(opposite page)

Giselle, Act II

Igor Youskevitch, Alicia, Nora Kaye, and Barbara Fallis in *Apollo*

Alicia with Igor Youskevitch in *La Fille Mal Gardée* (opposite page)

Alicia and Igor Youskevitch in *Theme and Variations*

Alicia and Igor Youskevitch in Bluebird Variation from *Sleeping Beauty*
(opposite page)

DANCE ROO

HEUTE

NR. 116 • MÜNCHEN, 2. AUGUST 1950 • 50 PF./1.50 SCH.

»Ballett-Theater«

Bildbericht in diesem Heft

Moderne Schatzsucher | Wie einst in der Pußta | Modespionage in Paris

Alicia and Youskevitch in *Romeo and Juliet*

Alicia with her mother and daughter Laura in Los Angeles, 1957
(opposite page)

Alicia and Youskevitch on cover of German magazine, *Heute*
(opposite page)

Alicia backstage in Paris, 1953, preparing to appear in _Theme and_
Variations

9

Ballet Alicia Alonso

$\mathcal{A}$fter the closing of Ballet Theatre, Alicia and Fernando invited the laid-off dancers to join them in Havana, where they quickly put together the performing company that they had dreamed of for years.

A decade before, they had first discussed organizing a small performing company with friends Maria Karnilova, Newcomb Rice, and a few other dancers, all of whom were passionate about ballet but had no place to perform. They had even hired a costumer and, through a friend, arranged their first booking in Caracas, Venezuela. But the project never materialized.

Over the years, Alicia and Fernando dusted off the idea and looked at it anew. Their own performing company! To dance when they wished, to choose their own roles, to avoid the painful wait to be selected—or not selected—for a role! These personal needs of the fledgling performers made up the early vision. By 1948, Alicia and Fernando were motivated by additional considerations, not only by the collapse of Ballet Theatre but also by their ties to Cuba, where they had deep family roots and where their daughter, Laura, was studying ballet at Pro Arte. Each year when Alicia danced at Pro Arte, she would remember that she took her first lessons there but then had to go to a foreign country to learn ballet technique. Now she saw promising youngsters at Pro Arte and she knew that without an opportunity to grow, their talent would wither.

In frequent interviews in the press, she expressed her hopes. "It is important to have a Cuban ballet company," she said, "for the Cuban is a person of warmth . . . with innate rhythm . . . and a true sense of the dance. . . . Here in Pro Arte, there are ballerinas who can consider themselves professionals but who have no opportunity to show it."

A showcase for Cuban talent—this was Alicia's and Fernando's dream. And like Lincoln Kirstein and Lucia Chase in the United States, they were also filled with a larger vision—to form a company that would reflect in style and content the Cubans' special attributes and traditions.

They had been building toward this moment over the years as they forged links between the provincial ballet in Havana and the vital dance forces in New York. Alicia and Fernando brought back to Havana each year not only their own improved skills but also their American ballet friends. They performed in classics restored by Alberto Alonso to their traditional choreography rather than the subjective fragments Yavorsky had staged. John Kriza, Maria Karnilova, André Eglevsky, Nora Kaye, Barbara Fallis, Marjorie Tallchief, and others joined Alicia and Fernando in highly professional productions.

(Distinguished companies had also appeared at Pro Arte. Anton Dolin performed there in 1946 with Markova, Rosella Hightower, and George Skibine. In 1947, Ballet Theatre visited Havana with a full company and repertory of dances.)

It was not only the classics that flourished in Havana but also avant-garde works created by Alberto Alonso. He had become director of Pro Arte Ballet School in order to express his broadened dance interests, including choreography. With other artists he explored the culture of the poor people, isolated by poverty and race, trying to fuse their African traditions with the cultural mainstream. Often the works of these artists caused a scandal. Typical was the 1947 ballet *Antes de Alba*, choreographed by Alberto Alonso with a modern score by Hilario González and modern design by Carlos Enriquez. Alicia created the role of a poor girl, the victim of poverty and prejudice, who commits suicide. Not only was the content shocking to an audience expecting a romantic diversion, but Alberto was also innovative in style, integrating the steps and rhythms of the conga and rumba into the classical ballet idiom.

These experiments by Cuban choreographers, the increasing awareness by Cubans of their own culture and talent and Alicia's growing prestige, all prompted Alicia and Fernando to seize the opportunity to launch Cuba's first ballet company when Ballet Theatre discharged its dancers.

They called it Ballet Alicia Alonso, using Alicia's name like a banner to rally support. In all walks—among the affluent, the educated, the poor—she was a beloved figure. Even when she had danced only small roles in New York, she was a star in Cuba. Each year she returned home, bringing her ripening gifts. The audience would greet her onstage with waves of applause and often break out into cheers.

Fernando Alonso became the new company's director; Alberto Alonso was for a time its artistic director; Alicia was the prima ballerina.

The company looked like a miniature Ballet Theatre in Havana. Of its forty members, only sixteen were Cubans. Most came from the United States, among them Igor Youskevitch, Barbara Fallis, Cynthia Riseley, Melissa Hayden, Helen Komarova, Paula Lloyd, Michael Maule, Royes Fernandez. Cubans Dulce Wohner (as Dulce Anaya she would become prima ballerina of the Stuttgart Ballet Company) and Enrique Martínez performed in principal roles. Other Cubans made up the corps de ballet. The musical directors were Ballet Theatre conductors Max Goberman and Ben Steinberg.

More than personnel was borrowed. Pro Arte generously lent the fledgling company toe shoes, costumes, sets, music, props. Its rehearsal halls and auditorium were rented for minimal fees.

The youthful company rehearsed a broad repertory of the classics, including *Giselle,* the Black Swan pas de deux, *Petrouchka,* and *Coppélia.* There were also modern ballets.

Enthusiasm and lively spirits held the company together. But capital—financial backing—was so minimal that Ballet Alicia Alonso had to fight to survive throughout its years of existence.

At the company's debut on October 28, 1948, the élite of government, society, and business filled the auditorium of Pro Arte to celebrate another milestone in Cuban ballet history. Alicia Alonso and Igor Youskevitch were the lead dancers in a demanding program that night and two subsequent nights which included the *Pas de Quatre, Swan Lake* Act II, *Giselle, Peter and the Wolf* and *Les Sylphides.*

With a small profit from these successful opening performances, the company fearlessly departed on its first Latin American tour. In

Caracas, the company performed several times with great artistic success—and then found itself in the midst of a state of siege. A military coup toppled the elected president. Armed militia, tanks, soldiers, patrolled the streets, barricading the company in its hotel. Undaunted by danger, many dancers rushed to the hotel roof to watch the fighting in the streets below. With the theater closed and the tickets unsold, the manager could not pay the ballet company. It meant unpaid hotel bills and often no money for food. But the dancers were saved from their predicament by the University of Puerto Rico at Río Piedras which chartered a plane to fly them out of Venezuela. In San Juan, the company gave five successful performances and was awarded the keys to the city.

Back in Cuba after a harrowing flight on a crippled plane, a few Americans left for safer shores. But with unexpected time on their hands because of the shortened Venezuelan tour, the rest of the company decided to tour the Cuban provinces, traveling by bus to remote towns and staying in local hotels. Crowds filled plazas and theaters to see the unheralded event—ballerinas in tutus, danseurs in exotic costumes. Most had never before seen ballet or even heard of it.

Before leaving on another tour of Latin America, Ballet Alicia Alonso gave three financially successful performances in Havana underwritten by government and by corporate business. One performance in the University of Havana stadium established an alliance with the student organization, the Federacion Estudiantil Universaria (F.E.U.) which would become a crucial source of support in later years. It also set the stage for additional popular performances in the vast stadium. Everyone wanted to see Alonso, Youskevitch, and Cuba's new company.

At one performance, 30,000 people, admitted free, jostled for space. After the gates were closed, thousands more wanted to get in. They began taking the gates apart. Permitted to enter, they rushed down the aisles to sit on the grass around the makeshift stage set up in the center of the field. Youskevitch felt the surging power in the throngs of people. He could see there was no place to walk, every aisle was clogged.

In the unbelievable quiet of that vast throng, the loud voice of one man sailed over the crowd annoying both the audience and the dancers. With the aisles jammed there was no way to usher him out. Quick as a flash, hands lifted him bodily out of his seat and passed him over people's heads to other raised hands and to still other hands until he was deposited outside the stadium gates.

In January 1949 the youthful enthusiasts in Ballet Alicia Alonso again took to the road, on an eleven-country trek through Central and South America that would last much of the year. Without funds to pay for publicity and to arrange bookings in large cities, the company was often forced into the cold neglected halls of small towns. Throughout, it was a beleaguered company, often short of funds for the barest necessities and dependent on ticket sales from each performance to send the dancers on to the next one.

Traveling with the company was Alicia's mother. Her father had died a few years before. He never did see her perform in New York. The night he was supposed to see her dance at the Metropolitan Opera House he was taken ill with a stroke and never fully recovered. Thereafter Alicia sent him movies of her dancing.

Alicia's mother, with her sense of design and ingenious skill with a needle, held the company's fraying costumes together. In a small town in Colombia, Alicia decided to fill in the schedule with a performance for the first time of the Fokine-Saint-Saëns *Dying Swan*. But she needed a costume. In her mother's room at the hotel, she complained about the shortage of money—even for fabric. Her mother, who had made all of Alicia's costumes, calmed her. "Don't worry," she said, "I'll think of something."

When Alicia returned from rehearsals, she saw her costume spread out on a chair. "How did you do this?" she laughed, fingering the wisps of delicate fabric.

Her mother teased Alicia for a moment, then told her to look at the long sheer curtains covering the windows.

"The curtains had very large double hems," she said, "I cut off part of the inside hem, resewed them, and got some fabric for your costume."

The dancers' debts mounted and their spirits often flagged but they pushed onward like pioneers opening up the frontier. In a way they did, stirring Hispanic pride throughout Latin America for the first company born in the Greater Antilles, the cluster of islands that includes Cuba. When North Americans left the company, talented Latin American dancers such as Lupe Serrano, Salvador Juarez, Felipe Segura, and Nicholas Magallanes replaced them.

And there was always the example of Alicia herself, infusing the company with her dynamism, expressing the ballets' meaning through her style and technique. In the process of leading the company, Alicia enlarged her own vision, exploring the classics for new meaning and reshaping them.

"Alicia Alonso has such stature as an artist, she can pass any test," said the newspaper *La Cronica* in Lima, Peru. "Even in the *Dying Swan* of Pavlova legend, Alonso gives it something new. Her swan is a thing of beauty."

In Mexico, the newspapers called her a ballerina of the Antilles, "whose perfect technique compares favorably to the best dancers of our time."

To keep the company going, Alicia and Fernando used their own savings, borrowed money, and urged the Cuban government to help.

The worst debacle occurred in Chile, where the company was stranded for a month. Even at a second-rate hotel their luggage was kept in lieu of payment. The Argentine government came to the rescue, chartering a plane to fly them from Chile to Buenos Aires and putting them up in hotels. Alicia and Fernando let it be known that a foreign government provided help while their own government ignored their appeals.

Though the tour was a financial disaster, the troup enjoyed great artistic triumphs. At its farewell performance in Buenos Aires, the company received an unprecedented nineteen-minute ovation.

In Havana, support organizations sprang up to help the battered company. A committee of students, an organization of distinguished women, everyone in the arts—all pressured the government of Prio Socarrás for a financial subsidy for Ballet Alicia Alonso.

The company, with its tattered costumes and scenery, could not accept important engagements abroad. Sol Hurok wanted to book them in the United States but the company's inflammable sets were an unacceptable fire hazard. Alicia added her voice in an appeal to the government. When she danced abroad, she said, she wanted to bring fame and glory to Cuba. "Does not our government—or the Cuban people—wish to gain prestige in the world?" she asked. To forestall its end, the company accepted all job offers, performing in local theaters and on television.

Finally, in 1950, the Ministry of Education provided Ballet Alicia Alonso with a monthly subsidy and a sum of money to pay off its most pressing debts. But after receiving their back wages, many members returned to their home countries, leaving Ballet Alicia Alonso temporarily short of personnel.

To prevent that from happening again, Alicia and Fernando opened their own school—Academia de Ballet Alicia Alonso—to train a new generation of Cuban ballet dancers.

The Academia, with Fernando as director and Cuca Martínez as assistant director, was housed in a renovated building in Vedado. They opened their doors wide to an untapped source of talent, offering scholarships to youngsters in public schools and orphanages who showed an aptitude for dance. There Cuba's outstanding dancers were trained. They include Mirta Plá, Josefina Méndez, Laura Alonso, Loipa Araujo, Aurora Bosch, Marta García, Ramona and Margarita de Saa.

Throughout all the turmoil Alicia never stopped dancing. So long as she was dancing she could cope with the unforeseen anxieties and pressures confronting her. It kept her whole psychologically and physically. In her simple direct way, she made it very clear. "I could not live if I did not dance," she said.

When it became certain that the government subsidy could not meet the company's continuing financial drain, Alicia decided to help subsidize it herself. In the fall of 1950, she returned to New York to join the reborn Ballet Theatre in time for its first tour of the European continent. Fernando, who had been with her in the United States at every stage of her career, remained in Cuba. He directed the company and, with Cuca, the school that bore Alicia's name.

She explained her deep commitment to the Cuban company in an interview in the magazine *Bohemia*. "I think," she said, "the artist has a social mission to fulfill and this mission must be realized in the service of the society in which one has been born and lives."

In undertaking the taxing schedule of performing with two companies, Alicia risked her health. She had no time to think about the doctors' caution: "Emotional stress as well as hard work will affect your eyes." But in the early 1950's the gradual erosion of her eyesight began; by the end of the decade it was seriously impaired.

Alicia was in the air as much as she was on the ground, flying from one engagement to another. "How else," she would say, "could I perform in London one night and be in Havana the next?"

In Havana, the Academia de Ballet Alicia Alonso and the Ballet Alicia Alonso continued to shape ballet into a vital artistic force. Fernando, an outstanding teacher, began his work on a system of pedagogy based on what he felt were the special attributes of the Cuban—the warmth, the natural muscular resilience, and the wide emotional range.

The regular staff, which included Fernando, Alicia, Cuca, and the Argentinian ballerina Carlotta Pereyra, was augmented by distinguished guest teachers. From England came Mary Skeaping, George Goncharov, Phyllis Bedells; and from the United States, Charles Dickson, Leon Fokine, and Alexandra Fedorova. Dickson, for a few years, was ballet master of Ballet Alicia Alonso.

The classics were refurbished. Alicia performed with André Eglevsky in a new production of *Giselle* staged by Fernando. She appeared with John Kriza in a new version of *Coppélia*. The French dancers Nathalie Philippart and Jean Babilée performed in Havana in Roland Petit's *El Joven y la Muerte* (known in the United States by its French name *Le Jeune Homme et la Mort*). For that production the Association of Theater and Film Editors in Havana gave Ballet Alicia Alonso an award. In 1953 Alicia staged a new production of *La Fille Mal Gardée*.

But the school and the company were not only building a Cuban style of dance and reshaping the classics. Ballet became an instrument for the expression of a new sense of nationalism surging through the country. Political forces were gathering to unseat Fulgencio Batista, who had become dictator in a military coup in 1952. Protests, strikes, and demonstrations were erupting in all parts of the country. Students were again marching down the streets demanding an end to repression. In July 1953 a young lawyer named Fidel Castro with more than a hundred followers, two of whom were women, stormed the Moncada Barracks in Santiago de Cuba. The attack failed, ending in the immediate death of many and the brutal torture of others. Only enraged public opinion saved a few of them for trial.

New works choreographed by Cubans—to music by Cuban composers and with sets and designs by Cuban artists—became popular. In 1953, to commemorate the hundredth anniversary of the death of the great Cuban patriot José Martí, Ballet Alicia Alonso presented *Versos y Bailes (Poems and Songs)*, inspired by four of Martí's most popular poems. The ballet, choreographed by Cuca Martínez, with music by Francisco Nugué, was a combination of poetry, dancing, and music.

By 1954, Ballet Alicia Alonso was 60 percent Cuban. For the first time, all members of the corps de ballet had entered the company from its own Academia. Their excellent dancing showed the results of Fernando's teaching methods. Among the principal dancers were outstanding Latin Americans—Carlotta Pereyra of Argentina, Víctor Alvarez of Uruguay, José Parés of Puerto Rico. The American-born and trained danseur Royes Fernandez became Alicia's partner.

That year the company undertook a successful four-month tour of Latin America. In one five-day period, Alicia performed in two productions of *Swan Lake*, as well as *Coppélia*, a deeply moving *Giselle* with Fernandez as Albrecht and Alicia's own psychological drama *Lydia*. Choreographed in 1951, this tragic story tells about a girl whose overzealous mother has crippled her development. From childhood, Lydia is in a cell in an asylum where she finally commits suicide. The starkness of the ballet is created not only by Alicia's dancing but by the decor and the haunting music of Nugué.

In 1955, with the company almost completely Cuban in composition, it was renamed Ballet de Cuba. Then in 1956, the government of Fulgencio Batista withdrew its subsidy, which had helped maintain the company. The government offered, instead, a small monthly remuneration to Alicia herself and some support for the Academia. Further, the government proposed to absorb Ballet de Cuba into its National Institute of Culture.

Alicia rejected all these proposals of the Batista government. She directed a letter to the Institute of Culture, subsequently made public, saying that the offer of remuneration for herself sounded like "charity" or "bribery" and that she would have no part of it; that the government withdrawal of support for the company was a blow to the artistic aspirations of the Cuban people; that when she asked for a subsidy, she did not intend the government to absorb the company; that she would not permit Ballet de Cuba to be deprived of its artistic independence and made an arm of government.

The government's action and Alicia's bold response aroused a storm of activity throughout the island, bringing Ballet de Cuba the support of leading cultural figures and mass organizations. A Committee for the Defense of Ballet was formed with prominent figures in theater, dance, television. Alicia became a public speaker. She toured the island with Ballet de Cuba and addressed the audience after each performance explaining the government's proposal and her response.

To honor and support Alicia Alonso in the face of the government's action, a giant rally was staged at the University of Havana stadium on September 16, 1956. It had been called jointly by the F.E.U., the student organization, and the Committee for the Defense of Ballet. Distinguished speakers honored the dancer in an outpouring of tribute. With her ballet company Alicia performed in *Les Sylphides*, and closed the spectacle with the *Dying Swan*.

The cheering and shouted "bravas" of 30,000 people paid tribute to Alicia Alonso and to Cuba's first ballet company. The company would never again perform in Cuba while the dictator Batista was in power.

10

Havana · New York · Moscow

*W*hen Alicia returned to Ballet Theatre in 1950, six years before the rally at the University of Havana, she faced a difficult period of adjustment. For two years she had been intensely preoccupied with ballet problems in Cuba. There she headed her own company and was a prima ballerina. In New York she was simply one of the principal dancers in the company. She had to find her niche again, and once more to wait her turn for leading roles. Ballet Theatre had divided them among the other principal dancers who had worked together since the company regrouped in 1949 with Nora Kaye, Nana Gollner, and Igor Youskevitch as well as Janet Reed, Muriel Bentley, John Kriza, and Hugh Laing.

Dance companies in the United States, as well as in Cuba, were appealing to government for support in order to survive. To make the 1950 European tour possible, the company was sponsored by the congressionally chartered American National Theater and Academy (ANTA) under the auspices of the State Department's Cultural Division. ANTA's sponsorship brought about the change of name to American Ballet Theatre.

The many new corps members and lead dancers hardly had adequate rehearsal time to fuse into a tightly knit ensemble before their departure. Nevertheless, with sixty dancers and technicians and fifteen tons of scenery and costumes, the company set off for a five-month tour of Europe in the summer of 1950, making twenty-one stops in eight countries. American Ballet Theatre performed before the U.S. Occupation Forces in West Germany, at the Edinburgh and

Venice festivals as well as in London, Rome, Genoa, Florence, Paris, and other European cities.

Audiences crowded into concert halls to see their first American ballet company. Again, as in London in 1946, American genre ballets received the most enthusiastic response, especially Agnes de Mille's *Rodeo* and Jerome Robbins's *Interplay*. Igor Youskevitch received unreserved affection for his dancing in the classics. Audiences remembered his elegant partnering of Danilova and Markova years before with Ballet Russe de Monte Carlo. Nora Kaye was a hit in *Pillar of Fire* and in *Giselle*. Alicia, who performed few lead roles, danced the Black Swan pas de deux with Youskevitch in Paris and brought down the house. Her Giselle drew an ovation and the Paris press said her performance captured much of the magic of the old ballet. At Scotland's Edinburgh Festival, however, a reviewer called her dancing "cold" and said it "seemed to detract from what might have been a wonderful performance."

On the company's return to New York, where she had not been seen since 1948, Walter Terry welcomed back "the ever brilliant Alicia Alonso." Her return was all the more fortuitous for within a couple of months American Ballet Theatre suffered a series of serious defections. Nora Kaye left for New York City Ballet, and Hugh Laing and Diana Adams also departed. Nana Gollner had made other arrangements before the European tour; so, too, had Antony Tudor, depriving American Ballet Theatre of most of his works. In the change, many thought Alicia Alonso was the one clear gain.

For the first half of the 1950's, four lead dancers held American Ballet Theatre together: Alicia Alonso, Igor Youskevitch, John Kriza, and the newly added, talented Mary Ellen Moylan. But the company depended primarily on the personal force of Alonso and Youskevitch. Out-of-town contracts were often signed only on the guarantee that they would perform.

Having found her place again in the American company, Alicia became the brilliant dancer critics and audience expected to see. That spring she did a winning *La Fille Mal Gardée*. Her performance as the Swan Queen at the Metropolitan was called by Walter Terry ". . . a miracle of beauty in line, in phrasing, in accent and in the accomplishments of feats and skills." Her Giselle left the audience cheering. "For the first time this season," wrote John Martin, "here was Alonso of old, the true ballerina, warm, brilliant and completely in command of her technique . . . doing a deeply touching mad scene."

That year the company premiered eight new ballets, and Alicia had the lead roles in more than half of them. In April she, Youskevitch, and Norma Vance premiered Ballet Theatre's first performance of William Dollar's *Constantia*, or *Concerto*, to music by Chopin. Critics said that Alonso and Youskevitch belonged singly and together to "the very great of the world of dance."

But not everything was golden. Alicia's own work, *Ensayo Sinfonico*, which she had created for Ballet Alicia Alonso to Brahms's "Variations on a Theme by Haydn" was half-heartedly praised by Terry as a "clean neat ballet." The *New Yorker* magazine called it a "succession of limp exercises." Another Cuban work created for Ballet Alicia Alonso—*Tropical Pas de Deux* of Enrique Martínez to music of Amadeo Roldán—did not fare any better.

Sometimes exhaustion caught up with Alicia, and Walter Terry noted after one performance that "her intensity . . . slumbered along with that of her partner."

These were minor setbacks barely affecting the continued acclaim. In September 1951 John Martin called Alicia Alonso "the grand ballerina . . . who can step up among the immortals." A month later, her name was listed first on the American Ballet Theatre program, the company's way of recognizing her prestige. That evening she created the leading role in Bronislava Nijinska's *Schuman Concerto*, the only new work that season.

In 1952, as her career soared, Alicia helped keep American Ballet Theatre alive by performing in the Warner Theater in New York between showings of a Western movie. The great ballerina danced the Pas de Sept and the Rose Adagio from *Princess Aurora* four times a day, sixty-four times in sixteen days, twice as often as she had danced them in her entire career.

By the end of the year, Alonso's dancing was dazzling. Martin said, "Her movement has a mystery of phrasing that she has never before approached." The *Saturday Review of Literature* stated: ". . . there comes a time when the act of dancing ceases to be a matter of muscular effort and seems to proceed from the body by direction of the mind.

. . . That moment came for Alicia Alonso in Black Swan pas de deux; . . . there was a surging sense of dance." The *Chicago American* dance critic Ann Barzel called her "the first woman of ballet without forgetting Fonteyn or Alicia Markova. All of them have art. But Alonso has virtuosity, temperament, versatility. She is the greatest virtuoso dancer before the public today."

Alicia fully hit the consciousness of the European public in American Ballet Theatre's tour in 1953. In Vienna, Alonso and Youskevitch were called "particularly outstanding." Berlin, cool to American Ballet Theatre, had praise only for Alonso and Youskevitch. In London, *Giselle* was hailed. The *Daily Express*, rapturous in its comments, said "Alicia Alonso . . . took London by storm. . . . When one sees Alicia Alonso, one understands why the American public is not unhappy when it does not often see Margot Fonteyn. She is technically faultless, dramatically strong and very human."

Her successes spiraled, never coming to rest even on some high plateau. And each performance became an adventure, for Alicia would always say that dancing a role was a continuously evolving process of interpretation. "You never, never stop learning," she said time and again. And she learned from everything she saw and heard—from acting, singing, painting, sculpture, or the everyday scenes around her, the way people walked, the timing of a step, the gesture of the hand, the tightening of a fist. At the theater she observed the way a performer delineated character with the line of head, neck, and body. Or she went to a museum to immerse herself in period painting to get the proper atmosphere for a classical role. She fed every new insight—every detail—into a role. To prepare for Juliet in Tudor's *Romeo and Juliet*, she studied Botticelli's paintings. At home, she stood before a mirror imitating the carriage and line of the women in the paintings. Or, to get the feeling of the classical line for Balanchine's *Apollo*, she looked at classical sculpture. Then she practiced standing like one of the statues—and when she felt comfortable in that position, she moved into the technique of ballet.

The dimensions of her personality were not evident on the surface. She appeared painfully shy on television in 1954, in a program called "This Is Your Life." Looking demure, gentle, with large dark eyes in a fragile face, she was genuinely touched and touching as her mother, sister, daughter, and husband, flown up from Cuba, and friends from New York, were brought out to join her.

Alicia worked hard but she also gave the company many light moments. Always late, she made trains and planes only with the help of friends who would barge into her hotel room to wake her and help her throw her clothes into valises. Sometimes she was hauled onto a departing train.

At one performance of *Swan Lake* with Youskevitch, the orchestra was playing in a quick tempo, much faster than usual. Youskevitch, proud that he could keep up with the increased speed, lifted Alicia once, twice, three times. He was doing fine, he thought. But Alicia, who felt as if she were going up and down on a broken elevator, whispered to Youskevitch, "You are handling me like a sack of potatoes." At first Youskevitch was hurt, then he laughed. When he put Alicia down, the two of them, with their backs to the audience, laughed so hard that they could not wait for the curtain to close.

On her flights to Cuba, when the plane stopped at Miami International Airport in Florida, she rushed over to a restaurant for a piece of "the best apple pie in America" even if it meant missing her Havana connection.

At home, with Laura and Fernando, in a Havana suburb, Alicia finally became a private person. She and her daughter would spend hours together, in a rush of excited talk, bridging the gap of long absences when only letters and phone calls kept them in touch. A hardship of Alicia's career was the separation from her daughter, especially in Laura's early years. To ease the pain of long separations, Alicia made frequent trips to Havana or she arranged to have Laura brought to New York. In 1953, when Laura was fifteen, she chose as a birthday gift a trip to Europe to join Alicia who was there on tour. Surrounded by artists throughout her life, Laura saw their single-minded dedication. She knew that in the pursuit of their art many had to make sacrifices. Yet she saw her mother not as a great ballerina but as a fun-loving woman.

Alicia would sit on the floor with her legs straight out and listen to classical music or watch television. Because of her poor eyesight, she could do little reading and had to give up painting, which had been a favorite hobby. Strewn like pieces of art on her dressing table were tiaras and crowns she had made for ballet roles. She gave them as gifts to ballet friends.

But even as Alicia reached the heights of success, she was faced with hard decisions.

In the fall of 1955, Alicia took a bold and surprising step. Concerned about the fate of her Cuban ballet company, she made the difficult decision to leave American Ballet Theatre to become prima ballerina with Ballet Russe de Monte Carlo for six months of the year. She would then perform with her Cuban company for the other six months.

American Ballet Theatre management did not expect Alonso's departure, especially since, only a few months before, Youskevitch had moved over to Ballet Russe to become its danseur noble and its artistic adviser and coordinator.

Alicia's decision was based not only on her need to perform with the Cuban company but by the renewed administrative maneuvering at American Ballet Theatre. Nora Kaye returned to the company in 1954. Lupe Serrano had been added. And management, eager to wean itself from dependence on Alonso and Youskevitch, was reducing Alicia's schedule of performances. And perhaps because she had risen from the ranks, she never received the publicity and courtesies accorded visiting celebrities.

The Ballet Russe de Monte Carlo that Alicia joined was not the same company it once had been. In the many conflicts and changes over the years, its prestige had waned. The stars of its great days—Danilova, Toumanova, Baronova, Massine, Riabouchinska—had retired, joined other companies, or become outstanding teachers. Without a home base, Ballet Russe remained a touring company, though a popular one with American audiences to whom it brought a roster of ballet classics.

Ballet Russe was managed by Sergei J. Denham, a former Russian banker and businessman. Denham was noted for his economies. But to keep his company in the public eye, he nevertheless offered high salaries to top performers like Maria Tallchief, the prima in the previous season. Denham paid Alicia Alonso far more than she had ever received and granted her the privileges due a prima—such as traveling by plane when the corps traveled by bus.

The change from American Ballet Theatre to Ballet Russe left Alicia without the tight structure that had defined her life. But it gave her freedom to explore other aspects of her artistry. Though Ballet Russe included such fine performers as maitre de ballet Frederic Franklin and principal dancers Nina Novak and Leon Danielian, it clearly revolved around Alonso and Youskevitch, her partner and the company's artistic director.

In the spring of 1956, Alicia and Youskevitch performed in a special season in Havana with Ballet de Cuba. They danced *Giselle*, a full-length *Swan Lake* recently staged by Mary Skeaping in which Youskevitch performed as Siegfried for the first time, and an equally demanding version of Prokofieff's *Romeo and Juliet* staged by Alberto Alonso. After rejoining Ballet Russe for the summer, they returned again to Havana to perform with Ballet de Cuba at the Blanquita Theater before an audience of six thousand. That September, Alicia's confrontation with the Batista government ended the existence of the Cuban company.

In the spring of 1957, Ballet Russe opened at the Metropolitan Opera House in New York for the first time in seven years. *Dance Magazine* heralded the event with the announcement that the company would be led by Igor Youskevitch, "the finest premier danseur noble in the world today," and joining him will be the "equally brilliant and beloved Alicia Alonso as guest prima ballerina."

For the event, Frederic Franklin and Alexandra Danilova were special guests. Danilova, absent from New York for many years and much loved for her bright, demi-caractère roles, received a rousing ovation. Alonso, equally popular, also received a wildly enthusiastic reception for *Giselle*.

Alonso's dancing with Ballet Russe was not always successful. Many of the problems were due to Denham's stringent economies. His policy of cutting corners and reducing the company's size to a minimum affected the general spirit. Dreary productions and a listless corps made it difficult for Alonso, though often brilliant herself, to raise the company's general level.

Youskevitch was especially enraged at Denham's habit of dropping the final curtain at 11:30 P.M. to avoid paying overtime even though a performance was still in progress. When it occurred in

Montreal, Canada, Youskevitch threatened to walk out. And when Denham brought the curtain down prematurely even in New York, it confirmed the decision of the two great stars to perform with Ballet Russe thereafter only as special guests.

In the fall of 1957, Alonso was invited to stage and perform in *Coppélia* at the 23,000-seat outdoor Greek Theater in Los Angeles. She had staged ballets in Cuba but this would be Alicia's first chance in the United States to express that broader aspect of her talent.

She arrived in Los Angeles with a group of Cuban dancers, members of the defunct Ballet de Cuba. Among them were her daughter Laura, who had studied at Pro Arte and the Academia Alicia Alonso, Mirta Plá, Josefina Méndez, Aurora Bosch, and an Argentinian dancer Marta Mahr. Her mother, part of her group, was the costumer.

In two weeks Alicia had to turn fifty dancers of widely varied training and background into a unified company. In the lead roles were André Eglevsky as Franz and the Danish pantomimist Niels Bjorn Larsen—flown in from Denmark—as Dr. Coppélius. To fill sixteen vacancies, Alicia called an audition to which two hundred young girls responded. Serious and elegant in a black dress with pearls, her hair parted in the center and combed back, Alicia sat behind a table for four hours giving each dancer her full attention.

With the orchestra under the direction of Ben Steinberg, the production of *Coppélia* ushered in a program of dance for a new civic, non-profit organization. In the successful five performances, Alonso was applauded not only for her own comic gifts as a light, adroit Swanilda and skillful mime, but for the production as well.

Capping Alonso's career at the end of 1957 was an unprecedented invitation to perform in the Soviet Union. She would be the first ballerina of the Western world to dance there. Fernando, also invited, would fly over from Cuba to join Alicia on the tour.

Though Soviet ballet had not yet been seen in the United States, tourists and critics had reported on its spectacular productions and its brilliant ballerinas Galina Ulanova and Maya Plisetskaya, among others. Building on their heritage from tsarist days and the Imperial ballet schools and theaters, the Kirov Ballet Company in Leningrad and the Bolshoi in Moscow maintained their hegemony as citadels of great ballet.

At that time, Cuba and the Soviet Union had no diplomatic relations and the United States had to serve as an intermediary. Alicia was invited as an American dancer through the Cuban Ambassador to the United States. But because she was a Cuban citizen, the American Embassy in the Soviet Union did not extend the customary hospitality of arranging receptions for so prestigious a visitor. Nevertheless, the host country provided appropriate fanfare for its honored guest. Never for a moment did Alicia Alonso feel deprived or neglected. On the contrary, her unusual success turned the planned three-week tour into ten weeks during which she and Fernando covered 17,000 miles.

In a repertory consisting of the full-length *Giselle* and *Swan Lake*, she performed in the opera houses of Moscow, Riga (Latvia), Kiev, and 33-below-zero Leningrad. Throughout, the Russian companies adjusted to her version of the classics.

She opened in *Giselle* on Christmas night, 1957, at the Bolshoi in Moscow. That afternoon she arrived for rehearsals and found the great hall filled. She thought she had misunderstood her schedule. But her hosts explained that the audience was made up of teachers, dancers, and students who had come to observe and study her style of dancing.

In Riga, members of the corps lifted Alonso onto their shoulders and carried her to her dressing room. The newspaper, *Voice of Riga*, wrote that in the role of Odette-Odile, "Miss Alonso left the audience gasping with the unforgettable impression of her sculptured poses." In Kiev, her popularity was so great she appeared on television. Throughout the tour, dancers, critics, and audiences hailed her for her talent and for her American training. Most impressive were her well-prepared characterizations and her impeccable technique. They found her Giselle different from theirs, "daring, convincing, stirring the emotions and captivating the audience. . . ." There was great appreciation for her dramatic talent, "the stability and preciseness of the smallest movements and the brio of her pirouettes."

Fernando was invited to teach a group of principal dancers the unsupported "American pirouette." He even gave private lessons to the venerated ballerina and teacher Dudinskaya.

When she was not performing, Alicia attended ballets. A high point of her tour was to find herself at the barre between Ulanova and Tikhomirnova in a class at the Bolshoi School.

"Dancers talked about dancing, not politics, like in the United States," she would tell American reporters.

Upon her return to the United States, Alonso found greater acclaim than ever.

Olga Maynard noted in her book, *The American Ballet*, that, added to Alicia's charm and artistry there is the "awe with which American ballet has regarded her since she captivated the Russian audience and critics. . . ."

In the fall of 1958, critics spoke of Alonso's "sheer radiance." She was "luminous. . . ." "There are honey curves of her arms. . . . She embodies all femininity, gentleness. Her entrechats are unequaled. . . ."

Word reached Alicia in Chicago on January 1, 1959, where she was performing with Ballet Russe, that the Batista dictatorship in Cuba had been overthrown. She learned that Fidel Castro had swept down from the mountains of Oriente Province with a battalion of followers and had established a revolutionary government in Cuba. Interviewed in the Chicago press a few days later, Alicia expressed her hope that the grave injustices in Cuba would come to an end.

In February 1959 *Dance Magazine* presented Alicia Alonso with its highest award, the Silver Trophy. At a flower-decorated table of honor at the New York Athletic Club, she sat with the American dancer Vera Zorina, mistress of ceremonies. Miss Zorina, in glowing tribute to Alicia Alonso, recalled to the assemblage of dancers, balletomanes, and critics that dance, like no other work, required "unrelenting practice [for which one must] have passion and fanaticism."

"It was only a technicality," she continued, that Alicia was the "first lady of the arts in Cuba, for nearly all her performing experience had been with American companies. . . . From corps de ballet of Ballet Theatre to become leading ballerina of the company, of Ballet Russe, and her own Ballet Alicia Alonso in Cuba" was quite a feat.

In 1958, continued Miss Zorina, Alicia Alonso "thrilled balletomanes and dancers of Russia [and became] the envy of every dancer for having danced there and having succeeded so magnificently. . . ."

The inscription on the award to Alicia read: *To Alicia Alonso for illuminating the purity of classic dance with her radiant warmth —a daz-*

zling combination which recently brought surprise and delight to still other audiences in Russia.

There was a special salute for Alicia as wife, mother and—as of that very month—grandmother.

Alicia's own remarks at the festivities were brief. She talked of her Russian trip and experience, summing it up with the comment that "dancing and dancers all over the world speak the same language of the arts."

Then, taking note that just a month earlier a new government had been established in Cuba, she expressed the hope that "the changes . . . will result in a new ballet company for the world."

Alicia with Hugo Guffanti in 1968 Cuban film production of *Swan Lake,*
Act III

Alicia with Azari Plisetski and Ballet Nacional de Cuba in *Swan Lake*
(opposite page)

Alicia and Jorge Esquivel in *Edipo Rey*

Alicia and Jorge Esquivel in *Carmen* (opposite page)

Alicia and Orlando Salgado after a performance of *Carmen*

Alicia in *Carmen,* produced by Cuban Film Institute (opposite page)   **135**

Alicia visiting the Escuela Nacional de Arte, Cubanacán, with prima ballerina Mirta Plá, ballet mistress of the class

Alicia with prima ballerinas Josefina Méndez and Mirta Plá at rehearsal, Ballet Nacional de Cuba (top)

Alicia taking class with Fernando (opposite page)

Alicia's daughter Laura and grandson Ivan in Havana

At home in Havana

Alicia with husband Pedro Simón in Mexico, 1977 (opposite page)

 140   Cubanacán, a complex of buildings housing the national schools of the arts

11

Ballet for Everyone

*F*or the first two years after the revolutionary change in Cuba's government, Alicia Alonso traveled back and forth freely between the United States and Cuba.

In America she continued to perform as guest artist with Ballet Russe de Monte Carlo and American Ballet Theatre.

In Cuba, she and Fernando gathered together the dispersed dancers and personnel of the Ballet de Cuba. Auditions for the new company in the summer of 1959 were open not only to Cuban dancers but also to dancers in the United States and Latin America. The judges, too, reflected the hope for broad, free cultural interchange. Panelists included Alexandra Danilova, English dance critic P. W. Manchester, American dance critic Ann Barzel, Igor Youskevitch, Alicia and Fernando, Marta Mahr, and Ana Leontieva, who had been with de Basil's Ballet Russe and had opened her own ballet school in Cuba.

In September 1959 the Cuban government announced a large annual subsidy for Ballet de Cuba. Thus, the newest ballet company in the Americas was launched, free from financial worries and with the artistic independence to work out its own future. In her capacity as artistic director of the company, of which Fernando was general director, Alicia had won a rare opportunity to express her creative talents. She knew from her experience in the United States that few such positions existed and that many dancers were frustrated in their search for artistic growth.

In addition to the new responsibilities for Cuban ballet, Alicia continued to make guest appearances. In the summer of 1959, she returned to New York to perform with Youskevitch and Ballet Russe de Monte Carlo for a week in Theater-in-the-Park. Thousands each night attended this popular entertainment at an open-air amphitheater in Central Park. Alicia's repertory with the American companies had become limited to the classics and on this occasion she performed in either the Black Swan pas de deux, Act II of *Swan Lake*, the *Don Quixote* pas de deux, or *Nutcracker*, Act II.

In October Alicia, Youskevitch, and the Cuban company toured Latin America for ten weeks, terminating with a performance at Havana's National Theater. The company had an expanded repertory, including works by Alberto Alonso, Ana Leontieva, and Enrique Martínez.

The year 1960 held great promise as a lighthearted Alicia Alonso, with Fernando and other cultural figures, continued to forge links between the dance scenes in Cuba and the rest of the world. It would turn out to be the first year of an intense and challenging decade for Alicia—a decade of both major achievement and great personal suffering.

In March Alicia helped usher in Havana's International Ballet Festival, the first for Cuba and for Latin America. Participating in twenty performances before packed houses were six companies and two soloists from the Bolshoi in Moscow. A highlight of the festival was *Swan Lake* performed by Ballet Nacional de Cuba with Nina Timofeyeva as Odette-Odile and Boris Khokhlov as the prince. Equally successful was American Ballet Theatre's presentation of *Fall River Legend* with Lupe Serrano. To celebrate the international gala, the U.S. Embassy and the Cuban Tourist Commission gave receptions, as did the embassies of Mexico and Venezuela whose companies performed.

On April 21 Alicia appeared in New York at American Ballet Theatre's twentieth anniversary celebration a week earlier than scheduled to replace an ailing Markova in *Giselle*. Royes Fernandez, in his first Albrecht in New York, replaced Erik Bruhn, absent with a foot injury. A wild ovation greeted Alicia when she appeared onstage at the Metropolitan Opera House, drowning out the first few bars of music. Responding to the audience's enthusiasm and warmth, she gave an unusually tender and moving performance. "She was a flawless technician—dancing with phenomenal lightness," Louis Biancolli wrote the next day in the *World-Telegram and Sun*. Walter Terry in the *Herald Tribune* remarked on the "electrifying speed of her traveling entrechats."

The next night she appeared with Igor Youskevitch in the pas de deux from *Don Quixote* and John Martin commented on her bravura dancing, the "slow and flowing pirouettes, her remarkable aplomb." During that week she also did *Pas de Quatre* and her own scheduled performance of *Giselle* with Igor Youskevitch.

With those memorable performances Alicia Alonso's dancing came to an end in the United States. Fifteen years would pass before she would again be seen in the country in which she started her career.

Politics was not Alicia's field. Deeply immersed in the world of dance and touring in new countries, she had not kept her eye on political developments and knew nothing of the bitter charges and countercharges exchanged between the United States and Cuba. But like a foot soldier at the edge of a battlefield, she was caught in the crossfire. At the end of 1960, the United States placed an embargo on all exports to Cuba except food and medical supplies, and in January 1961 President Dwight Eisenhower broke off diplomatic relations. Alicia Alonso, though invited to perform in the United States, was barred from returning by the Department of State. The protests of friends in the dance world were unavailing. Other countries, in South America and Western Europe, fell in behind the U.S. position and barred her for many years.

Alicia had been dreaming of a beautiful world and a bright future when this blow struck. All at once a vital part of her life ended. Cut off with the sharpness of a scalpel were friends, partners, audiences, companies. Gone were people she loved throughout the Western world. "One's heart has capacity for only a certain amount of people," she said. "And there were my many good friends in the United States whom I missed. My professional life developed there; I am part of the growth of ballet in the United States. You do not give and take and forget so easily."

In April 1961 an exile force supported by a U.S. intelligence agency, invaded Cuba at Playa Giron, or as it is popularly known, the Bay of Pigs. The quick defeat and capture of the invaders further froze diplomatic relations between the United States and Cuba. And Alicia Alonso disappeared from the pages of the United States press at the height of her career as if her life had inexplicably come to an end or as if, like Giselle, she had been a spirit and had vanished into the earth.

In Cuba, there was a similar blackout of news about the cultural life in the United States as if it, too, had become extinct.

Alicia, who had already tested her strength against overwhelming obstacles, faced a new challenge—to develop a vital Cuban ballet company isolated from what she considered its artistic nerve center, New York, and in a larger sense, the Western world.

She plowed back into Cuba her experience, energy, and determination. She envisioned for Cuba a great dance company, a dance school, and more—cultural education and opportunity for a long-deprived and poor population. She became a teacher, organizer, and administrator, demanding of everyone the same exhausting hard work and discipline with which she herself functioned.

For Ballet Nacional de Cuba, Alicia took over the Spanish-colonial townhouse next door to Pro Arte Musical. The former owner, Fernando's mother, Laura Rayneri de Alonso, had contributed the house and other real-estate holdings to the new Cuban government. Stately reception rooms, built around a patio, were turned into rehearsal hall, classrooms, offices, and workshops. As she still does today, Alicia took class there and worked with members of her company. In a handsome office, furnished with elegant antique furniture, she held meetings to plan for the dance company and for the cultural growth of the country.

Alicia always saw ballet as a wonderful outlet for the energy of young children, and as a universal means of self-expression. To make sure everyone, child and adult, would have an opportunity to study it or at least to appreciate it, groups of dancers spread out across the island. Traveling in trucks, jeeps, buses, and occasionally by plane, carrying portable stages, scenery, costumes, they made their way from Havana to the foothills of the Sierra Maestra in Oriente Province. These young dancers visited rural villages and fishing towns. They showed slides, lectured, danced, demonstrated the art of making toe shoes, and told ballet stories. They performed on makeshift stages at factory sites and in cane fields, in broken-down theaters, or on the bare ground. And they made ballet part of the consciousness of the people. For thousands just learning to read and write, the word ballet became part of the vocabulary.

The arts flourished in Cuba even while the economy suffered severe blows from the embargo by Western countries. People lined up for rationed food, tools were in short supply, machinery broke down with no replacements but, for one dollar, superb ballet performances could be seen at the best theaters in town.

Alicia and other dancers not only performed but also participated in the life of the people. They joined work brigades and helped plant vegetables, harvest oranges, and patrol the streets.

Through the years Alicia devised creative roles for dance, incorporating it into school curricula starting in nursery school and making it part of continuing education in evening classes for adults. She put on special dance productions for children and staged a fresh version of *Peter and the Wolf* for those in hospitals. With daughter Laura Alonso and in conjunction with the psychiatry department of children's hospitals, Alicia worked out a system called Psycho-Ballet to help disturbed children. A new magazine, *Cuba en el Ballet*, was begun to inform readers about dance around the world.

Today, children who are talented and interested in dance go through levels of dance education starting in the community at the vocational school. Those who succeed go on to the more professional provincial school. And those determined to make a career of dancing enter the National School of Ballet where a full curriculum includes academic subjects as well as music, languages, and dance.

To accommodate the flood of new talent, a complex of educational buildings of striking architectural design was built in 1962–63 on the site of a former country club outside Havana. Called Cubanacán, the island's aboriginal name, it houses the national schools of ballet, modern dance, painting and sculpture, music and theater. The government pays for the full education at Cubanacán as it does at all other schools. There, Fernando Alonso for many years directed the National School of Ballet which he and Alicia helped to create. He had long ago established a reputation as an outstanding teacher.

Basic to the Cuban school of dance is pure classical ballet technique. But suffusing it are the traits of the Cubans themselves. The tropical climate has made Cubans muscularly supple. They are vivid, expressive people and when they dance they touch the audience with their warmth. The interracial composition of the group and its distinctive features give the Cuban company a unique stamp, making it as different from North American companies as they are different from the Soviet or the English.

Havana always drew the great performers who appeared throughout the Americas on tour. Among others, the Romantic ballerina Fanny Elssler performed in Havana in the 1840s and Pavlova danced there in the early 1900s. But not until the 1930s, when Sociedad Pro Arte Musical sponsored a ballet school, did Cuba begin to develop a ballet history of its own. And this happened only because Alicia Alonso, Fernando Alonso and Alberto Alonso received their initial training at Pro Arte. After years of study abroad, they returned to Cuba and painstakingly made dance a vital part of Cuban cultural life.

Above all, Alicia Alonso became Cuba's contact with ballet tradition, with the Russian, Italian, French, English and United States schools which formed the basis for her dance education. Alicia had fused qualities from these schools into her personal style which in turn has become the core of the Cuban style of dance. Ballet students learn her flashing extensions and incredible balances. They learn her slow pirouette, the warm, sensuous adagio which is full of the enjoyment of the moment, and the quick burst into an allegro with its fast tempo and clean, sharp footwork. She has taught them how to make their arm movements expressive.

Alicia has taught Cubans how to approach a ballet, to see it as a functional whole, to know not only the steps but how one role relates to another.

In working on *Giselle*, the company explores the ballet's historical background and the customs of the era in which it was written. Dancers learn that it reflects a certain period and could not be written today. The class lines are explicit, making it clear that the prince *never* could marry a peasant girl. Today in the United States, some companies stage *Giselle* as if Albrecht, like England's King Edward VIII in 1936, might abdicate his royal heritage and marry a commoner.

In the Cuban version, however, the historical perspective illuminates the roles of Giselle and her mother. They are poor peasants and the film of *Giselle* made in 1963 actually shows the poverty of their cottage, the sparse furnishings, the crusts of bread on the table. One understands the mother's apprehension when the handsome stranger Albrecht woos her daughter. And one can see Giselle's uncertainty— her wonder, joy, and final acceptance of Albrecht's "love." There is logic to her grief and madness following the revelations of Albrecht's true identity for, completely unattainable to the frail Giselle, his duplicity strikes her full force—he was only trifling with her affections. It makes sense when villagers angrily thrust the guilty, torn Albrecht aside to permit the mother to fall over Giselle's body.

The classics, intrinsic to the company's repertory, are given the respect owed to valued traditional ballets. But choreographers, composers, and designers are encouraged to create new works. Programs are often filled out with inventive ballets reflecting historical struggles. The talented Enrique Martínez did *El Despertar (The Awakening)*, dealing with the Cuban Revolution. Another choreographer, V. Zaplin, did *Liberación*. Ana Leontieva created *Exorcismo*, based on the Salem witch hunts of colonial Massachusetts.

Alberto Alonso has remained Cuba's most prestigious, award-winning choreographer. One impressive work, *El Güije*, performed to electronic music, is based on an old Cuban folk tale and deals with the spirit of the river. His innovative *Carmen* to Bizet's music arranged by Russian composer Rodion Schedrin, deals with symbols of life and destiny. Originally created for Maya Plisetskaya and the Bolshoi, it has become one of Alicia's favorite roles. Alicia also does Jocasta in Jorge Lefebre's *Oedipo Rey (Oedipus Rex)*. There is José Parés's *Coral Horse* and ballets by Méndez, in particular the popular and charming *El río y el bosque (The River and the Forest)*.

In its first year, before the burst of new talent could enrich its schedule, Ballet Nacional de Cuba took to the road, traveling to seven Latin American countries. In the following year, it went to Mexico. In the winter of 1960–61, it made its first tour of the Socialist world, including the Chinese People's Republic, the German Democratic Republic, Poland, Czechoslovakia, the Soviet Union, and other countries. Leon Fokine, at one time associated with Ballet Alicia Alonso, signed on as ballet master for the tour.

The dancers were warmly received wherever they performed and the official courtesies and privileges extended to them were a new experience even for Alicia who, in over twenty years of touring, had never been so honored. She took time away from the company to perform in France at the eightieth birthday celebration of Pablo Picasso and to appear before 40,000 people in Calcutta as special delegate at the centennial celebration of the great Indian poet Rabindranath Tagore.

From 1961 to 1964, the company stayed at home to work on its technique and repertory and to secure its place in Cuban society. Then, breaking out of its hibernation, it gained world attention in 1964 at the First International Dance Festival in Varna, Bulgaria. At this small resort town on the Black Sea, an open air summer theater seating two thousand was made available for contestants from eleven countries. Galina Ulanova of the Soviet Union headed a panel of judges that included English dance writer Arnold Haskell, Serge Lifar (the dancer-choreographer who is Russian-born and trained but French by reputation and experience), and Alicia Alonso.

The Cubans created a sensation at Varna. Three of them—Mirta Plá, Josefina Méndez, and Rodolfo Rodriguez —won medals.

The Cubans continue to win honors through the many years of the Varna competition which has grown to include over one hundred contestants judged by the most prominent figures in the dance world. Medal winners have been the Hungarian entry Ivan Nagy, a Canadian entry Martine van Hamel, and the Russians Natalia Makarova and Mikhail Baryshnikov, all four of whom have since danced with American Ballet Theatre. In 1974 Fernando Bujones of American Ballet Theatre won a gold medal and thunderous applause for his spectacular technique.

The Cubans, always impressive, brightened the proceedings with their superb style. Any of them might have won a gold medal, reported Arnold Haskell. "They are magnificently schooled, superb in physique, exotic, stylish, and gloriously feminine," he said of the ballerinas. He called four of them—Mirta Plá, Loipa Araujo, Aurora Bosch, and Josefina Méndez—"Cuba's jewels."

Alicia Alonso's dynamic force was visible in every step of her company's progress. She is the most "amazing woman in the world of ballet; it's small wonder that everyone loves her," reported Janet Sinclair and Leo Kersley in *Dancing Times*, watching Alicia at Varna. "A strict disciplinarian, she can push her dancers to the point of exhaustion, and they will burst into rapid Spanish and shouts of laughter, relax and then begin all over again. . . ."

Varna was also a meeting place for old friends. Someone would always remark on what a loss it was that Alicia and her company could not perform in the United States.

In 1966, Ballet Nacional de Cuba broke the Western blockade, dancing in France for the first time in six years. In Paris, the company opened the Fourth International Festival of Dance, where Alicia won a gold medal—the Anna Pavlova prize—as best dancer.

In 1967, Alicia made another breakthrough when she appeared, at Anton Dolin's invitation, with Les Grand Ballets Canadiens at Expo '67 in Montreal. Friends, critics, dancers, Cuban exiles, and balletomanes from the United States, longing to see Alicia, traveled to Montreal. Among the visitors were Maria Karnilova, Walter Terry, Lucia Chase, Donald Saddler, Royes Fernandez, and Eleanor D'Antuono.

Karnilova arrived while Alicia was in rehearsal. Not wanting to interrupt her, she sat down in the back of the theater. Alicia learned she was there and she stopped the rehearsal, shrieking "Marusha!" as Karnilova is affectionately known to friends. Karnilova rushed down the aisle and in clothes hardly appropriate for the occasion, climbed up on the stage from the orchestra pit. The two friends embraced each other and wept.

In her dressing room as friends crowded around her, Alicia quipped, "If ever I have a heart attack, it won't be from overwork but from the emotion of seeing old friends."

The young ballerina Eleanor D'Antuono hovered on the edge of the group. She wanted to say hello but was reluctant to push her way forward through the prestigious assemblage surging around Alicia—her idol from Ballet Russe days. Alicia, told she was there, asked for the young dancer and embraced her. D'Antuono burst into tears, touched that Alicia remembered her and heartsick that this great ballerina could not dance in the United States. D'Antuono remained in Montreal for four days to take class with Alicia. Not only the classwork but Alicia's personal courage inspired her.

After the opening-night performance in Montreal, Alicia joined her friends for supper. She sat across a table from Lucia Chase, who found it an "absolute joy" to see Alicia. Alicia leaned over the narrow table and said to her friend, "Let me see you." She peered closely and said, "Yes, I can see you now."

Alicia was dancing at the height of her artistry. She was also almost totally blind.

12

Private Struggle

*D*uring the decade of the 1960's, recognized as one of the great ballerinas of the world, Alicia Alonso could see only shadows. Yet she was never considered a blind dancer. That was not her self-image nor anyone else's image of her. Her artistry and her near-blindness were two streams running side by side through the landscape of her life. Like any other ballerina she could launch herself on the stage and command it by her presence. Her interpretation of her roles became richer, deeper, like the many hues and layers of a fine painting. Some said her suffering made her a genius.

In 1941, detachment of the retina in both eyes had left her with impaired vision. For the next twelve years she had every reason to hope the difficulties were behind her. But in 1953 she became ill, dizzy. Again she almost suffered detachment of the retina. After a period of rest, she practiced spinning with her eyes closed to overcome the dizziness and she continued to dance. But she then discovered that cataracts, complicated by the earlier retina detachments, were slowly forming over the lenses of both eyes, obscuring her vision.

The clouds over her eyes thickened during the busy 1950's as Alicia toured with her own Cuban company, with American Ballet Theatre and with Ballet Russe. Her family knew Alicia could not see very well. One night at dinner, she asked her sister Cuca for another helping of food. "But you have food on your plate," Cuca replied. There were other incidents in later years. At a performance in Havana, at the García Lorca Theater, she danced with her back to the audience. At another time, an electrical failure blacked out the theater but Alicia continued to dance.

In 1958 while performing in *Swan Lake* in Kiev, she tripped and fell backstage, suffering a severe cut near her right eye. The members of the company knew of her eye problems and were alarmed but Alicia insisted on completing her performance. Doctors there and in Moscow studied, checked, and tested her eyes. They could tell her nothing she did not already know.

By 1961, when the United States and Cuba broke off relations, Alicia Alonso was suffering the misery of going blind unknown to American friends. In Cuba a silent brigade of helping hands sprang up around her. No one said anything but someone was nearby at all times.

Doctors, friends, family—they all said her career was finished. How could she dance if she was blind? But Alicia never thought of herself as finished. To her it meant she had to work harder. Blindness was something to overcome.

Each morning Alicia took a lesson with Fernando. In the afternoon she worked alone, putting in a full hour en pointes, making up a challenging combination of steps to master. They were not only automatic, physical exercises but also mental exercises, impressing the steps into her consciousness.

When Alicia lost her sense of space and could no longer see into the distance of the stage, she relied on her inner image of a dance. She had developed that inner vision after eye surgery in 1941 when she lay in bed with bandaged eyes for most of a year. She had trained herself then to observe—with her mind's eye—the way she danced, as if she were in the audience. Part of her was performer, part of her observer. Now she stretched this inner vision again and, with phenomenal will, turned a physical disability into artistic strength.

Her dancing began to glow. In all movements—slow, poetic, or rapid like the rush of a waterfall—she made every inch of her body expressive, from her toes to the ends of her bony, sensitive fingers. Her arms, the port de bras, became eloquent. She could show character with the turn of a head or the flex of a wrist. And each gesture was true, with the absolute verity of a perfectly tuned instrument. Like a musical chord suspended in a room before slowly dying away, the nuances of her dancing clung to one's memory long after a performance.

Alicia's partners in the early years knew she could not see out of the corners of her eyes. Often Igor Youskevitch, in preparation for a lift, would see Alicia turn and run toward him in a curve rather than a straight line, making it difficult for him to get set. He would make a clicking sound so that she could judge where he was standing.

In the 1960's when Alicia was nearly blind, she painstakingly measured every movement of her body so that her partner would know exactly where she was going to be and what she was going to do. She had to have absolute trust in her partners to leap and soar in darkness.

Azari Plisetski, a Soviet-trained dancer and brother of Maya Plisetskaya, was Alicia's partner from 1963 to 1973. The technically strong Plisetski gave Alicia the full support she needed. Since 1974 she has danced with Cuban-trained Jorge Esquivel, a medal winner at Varna. "A beautiful partner," Alicia calls Esquivel, "with such strength, he makes you feel like a feather."

Long before rehearsal time, Alicia would get to the theater to find her bearings onstage. She had to adapt to an intricate system of chalk marks and light clues that showed her where she should stand and move. She also created her own devices. When, as Giselle, she must return to the grave, she would feel her way with her foot in order not to trip over the gravesite. Anton Dolin, sitting with Lucia Chase in the orchestra watching Alicia do *Giselle* in Montreal in 1967, excused himself for the second act so he could be in the wings with a flashlight to guide her offstage. With the stage covered with flowers and with the audience cheering her "to the rafters," Dolin placed a wreath around Alicia's neck.

Alicia's blindness was revealed to visitors from the United States at that performance. "Nearly Blind Ballerina, Cuba's Alicia Alonso, Wows 'Em in Montreal" headlined *Variety*: ". . . it was dancing . . . perhaps unparalleled in the history of the celebrated role. . . . There are no words for the emotional intensity of the standing ovation," it said.

The Toronto *Daily Star* reviewer commented: "Miss Alonso has been blind for a long time. Those large luminous eyes have no sight. She is aware of her fellow dancers by touch and sound. She responds to, as it were, vibrations from the floor. . . . She has not allowed the need to live in darkness to prevent her from continuing and growing in her profession."

In 1967, Alicia performed at the Festival of Paris and the next year at the Cultural Olympics in Mexico, where she won a medal. That year, Arnold Haskell, in his visit to Cuba, watched Alicia rehearse. "She is prodigious," he said. "I watch her every morning at rehearsal. Every muscle, every bone is solid, supple, responsive, in its prime. And she is one of the finest actresses we have today in ballet."

In 1969, Alicia went on an extensive tour that included the Soviet Union, Rumania, Bulgaria, and East Germany as well as Belgium, Holland, and Spain. In Moscow, Alonso was a juror for the International Ballet Competition at the Bolshoi. To observe dancers, she used powerful binoculars as she did at Varna and when she worked with her company.

Anges de Mille, also a juror at Moscow, had not seen Alonso for many years. She marveled that Alonso continued to dance though she could not even see de Mille's hand extended to her across a table. "Who can explain," de Mille said in amazement, "how she manages solos when she must launch herself leaping and twisting into blurred space, without guide as to direction or distance? . . . What incomparable bravery. She has the most beautiful feet in the business. These days they bear not only wings but laurels for valor."

In Copenhagen, Alonso danced with the Danish company where Flemming Flindt performed Albrecht to her Giselle. During rehearsals, Alicia crashed into the scenery and was almost knocked unconscious. Flindt, concerned, hovered over her and, with the rest of the cast, carefully worked out minute details to assure her safety. In Act II, Flindt took hold of Alicia and guided her to the flowers she must pick up. Dancers stood in the wings, tears rolling down their faces, watching a near-blind Alicia soar over the stage in a magnificent and touching performance. Janet Sinclair wrote that Alonso is "probably the world's greatest ballerina . . . her Giselle is as overwhelming as Ulanova's." Alonso, Sinclair said, was "suffering from near-blindness and refuses to give up." But that year, 1969, Alonso performed in the Black Swan for the last time. She could no longer spot, or focus, and do the multiple fouettés. In 1970, Alicia received the Grand Prix de la Ville de Paris jointly with her company at the Paris Dance Festival. In 1971, Alicia and the company danced in Montreal, and again friends, reviewers, and balletomanes made the pilgrimage from the United States to see her. Clive Barnes, who had last seen Alonso in 1953, wrote he had never expected genius ". . . but this has happened." Gerald Fitzgerald commented in *Dance Magazine*: "She creates miracles; her near-blindness has lead to artistic greatness." Alicia Alonso had become a dancer of history.

The interracial Cuban company, with its superb training, also earned high praise. It was beyond belief, reviewers commented, that a small underdeveloped country could provide one of the great ballet companies of the world.

For dancers, wrote Sinclair and Kersley, "Cuba is the promised land."

By 1972, Alicia Alonso could barely see a pinpoint of light. Only a voice could now guide her offstage. That year she toured and danced as if the Furies were at her heels. In February, she staged her version of *Giselle* for the Paris Opera and appeared in it for five performances. In Brussels she danced with the Maurice Béjart Company. To honor Alicia, Béjart added a classic ballet to the program usually made up of modern and avant-garde works. Partnered by the Italian danseur, Paolo Bortoluzzi, she did *Swan Lake*, Act II.

Béjart remarked of the fifty-one-year-old Alicia, "She defies time as well as nature." When reviewers asked her whether she planned to stop dancing, her reply was, "No, I am not tired."

But by fall, Alicia knew she could no longer put off eye surgery. For years she had resisted it, fearful that at her age prolonged absence from the daily routines at the barre would end her life as a dancer. When her doctor insisted that the eye damage might become irreversible, she had to submit to his decision.

That fall she flew with her company from Cuba to Prague. While the company continued on its tour to East Germany, she flew to Tokyo with Plisetski to appear in *Carmen* with the Tokyo Ballet Company. She rejoined the Cuban company in Budapest. But when it continued on to the Soviet Union and Bulgaria, where nine dancers picked up awards at the Dance Festival, Alicia flew to Barcelona. There, with her personal physician Dr. (Othon) Gómez Ruiz in attendance, she entered a clinic. The noted ophthalmologic surgeon Dr. Joaquín Barraguer operated on her eyes.

When the bandages were removed, Alicia had regained partial vision in one eye. The other was permanently blind. "A whole new colorful world has opened up," she remarked. "It is wonderful to see green salads again." Then she said, "Now I am ready to start my life all over again."

But as she had anticipated, it took the full force of her willpower to make the adjustments. She had danced sightless for over a decade. Now she had to adjust to dancing with partial eyesight.

"Well, now, surely you cannot dance," everyone said. Dr. Barranguer, too, predicted that at her age, she would never regain a sense of balance.

It seemed to Alicia that ever since she started her career, someone was telling her she could not dance. "I could not see doing any harm with my dancing. I thought I was giving people something beautiful in life—good memories, happy ones. So I did not see why I should stop dancing. That is why I kept on working to overcome all obstacles," she said.

But it was more than making people happy. It filled her own compelling need. For the two years she did not dance, Alicia became a sorely distressed person, sad, difficult, easily hurt, and given to outbursts of anger.

She broadened her activity in Cuba, mapping out curricula for schools, factories, for the handicapped, for the retarded. She joined more committees, worked in more organizations, chaired meetings.

In November 1973 Havana University awarded her an honorary doctorate in the arts, the first since its founding in 1728.

In 1974 she staged *Sleeping Beauty* for the Paris Opera. She continued to judge contests in the Soviet Union, France, Bulgaria, and Japan. In Cuba she worked on the Fourth Festival of Dance, at which Cynthia Gregory and Ted Kivitt of American Ballet Theatre became the first Americans to perform in Havana since 1960. People lined up for tickets the night before the performance, sleeping in the streets, to wait for the theater to open. A thunderous ovation greeted the two Americans. With Ballet Nacional de Cuba, they did *Coppélia* and *Swan Lake*. Gregory and Jorge Esquivel danced in *Apollo*.

In November 1974, at ceremonies paying homage to women, Alonso was given the Ana Betancourt award, named after Cuba's first woman fighter for women's rights. At the ceremonies, Alicia surprised the people of Cuba. She danced. Without telling anyone, friends or family, she had secretly rehearsed with the choreographer Alberto Méndez and with Jorge Esquivel, her partner. The simple number she did, *Las Mujeres (The Women)*, brought her back to the stage after a two-year absence. She had learned to keep her balance with partial vision in one eye.

Alicia worked on her repertory, learning, like an elementary schoolchild, how to keep her balance in works that had been part of her repertoire in the many years of darkness. In 1975, she did Jocasta in *Oedipo Rey*. Toward the end of the year, she could again do *Carmen*.

In the United States, Lucia Chase pressed the State Department to grant Alicia Alonso permission to appear at an American Ballet Theatre gala. When again the request was turned down in early 1975, Donald Saddler had the company tape a message to Alicia in Havana expressing their best wishes and the hope that she soon would be with them.

And then it happened.

The State Department reversed itself and granted Alicia Alonso permission to dance again in the United States.

Television program *This Is Your Life*, 1954. Alicia and Fernando, seated;
Ralph Edwards, master of ceremonies, Alicia's mother, Lucia Chase,
Alicia's daughter Laura, Igor Youskevitch, ballet teacher Alexandra
Fedorova, and nurse Ethel Prichard

Alicia backstage holding Cuban government medal of honor, the Order
of Carlos Manuel de Céspedes, awarded 1947 (opposite page)

Stamps commemorating the V International Festival of Dance, Havana, Cuba, 1976

A Cuban stamp honoring Alicia (opposite page)

French ballerina Lyane Daydé, Azari Plisetski, Alicia, Serge Lifar, and ballet teacher Boris Kniasef at the IV International Dance Festival, Paris, 1966

Alicia receiving honorary Doctorate of Arts from University of Havana Director Hermes Herrera (opposite page)

Alicia after performance, American Ballet Theatre Gala, 1975

Alicia with Margot Fonteyn and Maya Plisetskaya at Gala Performance of Tokyo Ballet, 1976 (opposite page, top)

Alicia at 1975 American Ballet Theatre Gala with Cynthia Gregory, Erik Bruhn, Cuban partner Jorge Esquivel, Ivan Nagy, Gelsey Kirkland, Fernando Bujones, Eleanor D'Antuono, and other members of the company (opposite page, bottom)

Alicia Alonso

13

Homage to Alicia

$\mathcal{A}$licia danced in New York in July 1975, after an absence of fifteen years.

Her appearance with Jorge Esquivel at the American Ballet Theatre Gala in the New York State Theater at Lincoln Center was a pas de deux that shook the world. Newspaper reporters who had never before seen ballet fought for tickets. They filed reports to capitals around the globe—to Paris, Rome, Peking, Moscow, London, Caracas. Her return to New York was more than that of a beloved ballerina. She was a harbinger of astounding political news—a first step toward renewed diplomatic relations between the United States and Cuba.

For Alicia and for her performance with Esquivel in the White Swan pas de deux from the third act of *Swan Lake*, there was a twenty-minute standing ovation filled with cheers and tears. From the balcony a banner was unfurled: "Welcome, Alicia, *Bienvenida!*" Rhythmic chants of "Alicia, Alicia, Alicia" shook the hall. Deeply moved by the rousing reception, and at performing again in a country she loved, Alicia took deep bows with tear-filled eyes.

Her brilliant, moving performance brought an overwhelming response. "It was Alonso's gala," wrote Clive Barnes in the *Times*. *El Nacional* of Caracas hailed her "technique and exquisite grace of movement. . . ." "Extraordinary!" said Mexico City's *El Universel*. The *Washington Post* critic wrote: "I seriously doubt that any other ballerina, regardless of age, could have interpreted the adagio from the White Swan with the range and depth of feeling shown by

Alonso. . . ." *Time* magazine talked about the "legendary ballerina." The *Los Angeles Times* called it "a moving and memorable night . . . her Odette is an ageless creature. . . ." In San Francisco they said "Alonso is timeless."

Three years after her own dramatic return, Alicia Alonso brought to the United States the company of which she is cofounder, director and prima ballerina. The Ballet Nacional de Cuba made its first appearance in New York at the Metropolitan Opera House in June, 1978. In the company of eighty-five were her grandson Ivan, a corps member, and her daughter Laura, a ballet mistress.

At every level the company justified the high praise it had received in other parts of the world. The program of classics and modern ballet revealed to audiences the high technical achievements of the dancers and their dramatic skill, as well as the clarity of each production that brought logic to their roles.

Outstanding among the many ballets premiered was *Blood Wedding*, based on a García Lorca play and choreographed by the Spanish dancer Antonio Gades, a special guest of the Cuban company. This tightly knit dramatic ballet, performed in flamenco-style dancing, showed the tensions and tragedy inherent in the narrow morality of a conservative Spanish family.

Equally successful, though of a different caliber, was *Canto Vital*, choreographed by Azari Plisetski and danced by Cuba's remarkable male dancers. Lazaro Carreño, Jorge Esquivel, Orlando Salgado and Andrés Williams displayed their virtuosity and reveled in the vigorous dance movement.

There was also *Paso a Tres*, choreographed by Alberto Méndez, in which Jorge Esquivel partnered two young dancers in a spoof of the traditional pas de deux.

Contributing to the success of the programs were Cuba's well-known ballerinas Loipa Araujo, Aurora Bosch, Marta García, María Elena Llorente, Josefina Méndez, and Mirta Plá, as well as many soloists obviously ready to step into leading roles.

Glittering as many performances were, nothing equalled the riveting quality of Alicia Alonso herself. Performing in the familiarity of her own company, with its intimate, almost organic sense of unity, she revealed her depth of feeling and the range of her artistry. She danced in *Giselle*, *Carmen*, *Oedipus Rex*, the pas de deux of *Swan Lake* Act II, *Pas de Quatre*, and in the premiere of Méndez' *Ad Libitum*, an amusing ballet contrasting the classical dance steps of Alonso with the flamenco dancing of Antonio Gades.

In *Giselle*, which Alonso has been closely identified with since 1943, she gave a "monumental performance," to quote dance critic Clive Barnes. *New York Times* dance writer Anna Kisselgoff called Alonso's staging of *Giselle* an "outstanding introduction to the meaning of Romantic ballet."

In *Carmen* Alonso commanded the stage with a thrilling performance and held the audience spellbound. She was sensuous and bold, slashing the air with her inimitable extensions. Her great dramatic skill gave credence to this difficult role. She swept the hushed audience along with her as she mockingly enticed her lovers and met her tragic end in the bull ring. Alonso was ageless, eternal. The wildly cheering crowd, moved by her memorable performance, all but leaped to the stage to shower her with love and admiration.

Alicia Alonso continues to shake up the world. She runs through the Stop signs established by custom as if they did not exist. Those social imperatives that place limits on one's activities have no meaning for her. Acting out of inner need and conviction, she has stubbornly shaped her own life. In doing so she has stretched the outer periphery of human capability for herself and for those who follow her. In young womanhood she swept aside cultural traditions that would have confined her to home and family. In the same way, she refuses to accept society's limitation of age on her dancing. Dancing when almost blind? She inspires thousands.

"You are a fanatic about dancing," Ulanova said to her.

"I like to dance," was Alonso's simple answer.

When a *New York Times* reporter recently asked her why she dances with such an infirmity, Alicia replied, "I know people say, Why doesn't she retire and be happy? I go on dancing because it makes me feel good mentally and physically when I dance. It is a necessary thing. So far my body demands it—and so does my mind."

There have been changes in Alonso's private life—in early 1974 a divorce from Fernando and marriage to dance editor Pedro Simon. At home, with Pedro and frequent visitors Laura and grandson Ivan, a gifted ballet dancer, Alicia will often show visitors a toe shoe that once belonged to Pavlova and which is now part of her ballet memorabilia.

Alicia says that wherever she has gone and traveled in the world, one dancer was there before her—Pavlova. "And there were no planes in those days," she says. "Pavlova traveled by horse, by camel, on foot. Every place I have gone, she has been there. Very few people have done as much for ballet," she says with great admiration. "She has been all over the world with her dancing, sometimes dancing the most difficult thing, sometimes the easiest. But always Pavlova had art—such an art that people have never forgotten her."

So Alonso, too, will never be forgotten. She has given of herself fully to every country in which she has danced. And every dancer will remember the rich experience of sharing the stage with her. In Cuba she leaves a legacy, the renowned Ballet Nacional de Cuba. And on the international world of dance she has already left her mark. She ranks with the great ballerinas of all time, with Karsavina, Ulanova, Plisetskaya, Fonteyn, Chauviré—with Pavlova herself.

Alonso was once asked why she, a universal star, stayed on in Cuba.

"By staying in Cuba," she replied, "I gained the love of my people. And who has that is very rich."

Explanation of Dance Terms
Selected Bibliography
Photo Credits
Index

Explanation of Dance Terms

ADAGIO Any slow dance movement. Also, a supported dance in which the ballet dancer, with the help of a partner, displays graceful, lyrical movement.

ALLEGRO A dance to a fast tempo.

ARABESQUE A ballet position in which the dancer stands on one leg and extends the other straight in back to form a long line from finger tips to toe. Position of arms varies.

ATTITUDE A ballet position in which the dancer stands on one leg with the other extended in back (or in front) bent at the knee.

BALLERINA A leading female dancer in a ballet company.

BARRE A wooden railing fastened to a wall which helps a dancer maintain balance.

BATTERIE Applies to all movements in which feet and legs beat together, usually in the air.

CARACTÈRE or

CHARACTER DANCER A term used to describe a dancer who performs folk or national dances (such as a gypsy dance) in a ballet; also to describe a clearly defined personality in a dance, like Dr. Coppélius in *Coppélia*.

CORPS DE BALLET The group or ensemble dancers of a ballet company.

CORYPHÉE A minor soloist.

DANSEUR NOBLE A classical male dancer and partner to the ballerina.

DEMI-PLIÉ See Plié

DIVERTISSEMENT A short dance, complete in itself, calculated to display the talents of individual or groups of dancers.

ELEVATION The capacity of a dancer to attain height in springing steps.

ENTRECHAT A spring into the air during which dancer rapidly crosses legs before and behind each other.

EXTENSION   The ability of a dancer to raise and hold an extended leg in the air.

FIVE POSITIONS   The basic positions of the feet in classical ballet which begin and end every step or movement.

FOUETTÉ   The dancer stands on one leg and is whipped around into a turn or series of turns with the other.

JETÉ   A jump in which dancer springs from one foot into the air and lands on the other foot.

LIFT   The upward or forward lift of a ballet dancer by her male partner.

LINE   The outline of a dancer with arms, legs, and head in harmonious relation to the body.

PAS DE DEUX   A dance for two persons.

PAS DE QUATRE   A dance for four persons.

PAS DE SEPT   A dance for seven persons.

PAS DE TROIS   A dance for three persons.

PIROUETTE   A full turn of the body on one foot usually done on half or full point.

PLIÉ   A bending of the knees. DEMI-PLIÉ, a small knee bend.

POINT, EN POINTE or

SUR LES POINTES To dance on the extreme tips of the toes.

PORT DE BRAS   Movement and position of the arms.

TURNOUT   A body position in which legs are turned out from the hip joint.

TUTU   A ballet skirt, made usually of layers of nylon or tarlatan.

VARIATION   An elaboration of a previously stated theme. Also a solo dance.

Selected Bibliography

For further research on Alicia Alonso, there are folders of reviews and articles, folders of photographs, and films in the Dance Collection, New York Public Library. There is also Tana de Gámez's *Alicia Alonso at Home and Abroad.* New York: Citadel Press, 1971.

For reading about ballet in general, any of the works of the following authors will be helpful: George Amberg, Clive Barnes, Edwin Denby, Agnes de Mille, Arnold Haskell, Lincoln Kirstein, John Martin, Olga Maynard, Walter Terry.

Also the following magazines: *Ballet Review, Ballet Today, Cuba en el ballet, Dance and Dancers, Dance Digest, Dance Magazine, Dance News, Dance Perspective, Dancing Times. (Dance Digest* and *Dance Perspective* are only available in libraries.)

For ballet summaries, see:

Balanchine, George, and Mason, Francis. *101 Stories of the Great Ballets.* New York: Doubleday & Co., 1975.

Krokover, Rosalyn. *The New Borzoi Book of Ballets.* New York: Knopf, 1956.

Terry, Walter. *Ballet Guide.* New York: Dodd, Mead & Co., 1976.

For references, see:

Chujoy, Anatole, and Manchester, P.W. *The Dance Encyclopedia.* New York: Simon and Schuster, 1967.

Clarke, Mary, and Vaughan, David. *The Encyclopedia of Dance and Ballet.* New York: G.P. Putnam's Sons, 1977.

Koegler, Horst. *The Concise Oxford Dictionary of Ballet.* London: Oxford University Press, 1977.

Wilson, G.B.L. *A Dictionary of Ballet.* New York: Theatre Arts Books, 1974.

Photo Credits

Dance Collection American Ballet Theatre
Dance Collection Ballet Nacional de Cuba
Dance Collection New York Public Library, Lincoln Center
Collection of Cuca Martínez-Hoyo
Collection of Norberto Sánchez
Tricontinental Film Center
Miriam Valente, Executrix Estate of Alfredo Valente

And a distinguished list of photographers who made their work available:

Luis Castañeda	94, 95
Eileen Darby	56
Beverley Gallegos	133
Tana de Gámez	137, 138 (top)
Giacomelli of Venice	66
Dwight Godwin	100
Leovigildo-González	163
Tonatihu Gutiérrez	139
George Karger	93
Michael Kidd	66 (top)
Bil Leidersdorf	164
Louis Mélançon	60
Walter E. Owen	105, 160
Louis Péres	165 (bottom), 166
William Reilly	135
Maurice Seymour	jacket, 53, 61
W.H. Stephan	97
Alfredo Valente	55, 58, 65, 103

Illustrations by Rene Portocarrero appear on pages 25, 51, 91, 129, 157

Index

• •